JN089229

はしがき

■この教科書と作者について

　この教科書は、ジャーナリスト、小説家、大学教師として活躍しているマイケル・W・ラーソンの中編小説 Notes on Brotherhood (2022) の全文を註とともに読みながら、合わせて読解前、読解後のタスクを行うことで、読解力を中心に、総合的な英語力を養えるように編纂されたものです。

　この作品はラーソン氏の自伝的小説で、1990年代から2000年代初頭にかけての少年〜青年時代を描いた短編小説の連作で構成されています。なお、タイトルの "Notes" とは、「覚え書き、メモ、記録」の意味で、"Brotherhood" とは「兄弟であること、兄弟というもの」を指しています。

　2005年の初来日以来、日本とアメリカを行ったり来たりしながら、ジャーナリスト、作家、研究者として活躍しているラーソン氏は、日本での滞在歴が通算10年以上にもなり、現在も日本の大学で教鞭をとっています。そういう事情もあり、この教科書のために Notes on Brotherhood を書き下ろしていただきました。

■この教科書とのつきあいかた

　各ユニットの前後にあるタスクについては、先生の指示にしたがってください。ここでは、本体となっている小説との向き合いかたについて、お話しします。

　各ユニットの読みかたは人それぞれではありますが、お勧めの読みかたは以下のとおりです。

1. まず註を参照しながら各ユニット全体に目を通す。このときは、少々わからないところがあっても飛ばしてかまいません。話の全体の流れをつかむのが目的です。
2. 次に、今度は、必要に応じて辞書を引きながら、ゆっくり読んでみます。あとでお話しするように、表現のされかたや会話の意味について考えながら読みましょう。
3. さらに、作品に出てくる文化的事象について、参考書やサイトで調べながら読んでください。Pre-reading で指示されている場合もありますが、それ以外のものについても積極的に調べましょう。
4. Discussion や Writing のタスクを手がかりに、自分の反応を言葉にするように努力してください。ここまでできて、初めて「読む」ことが完了すると言えます。

以下、これらの読みかたをお勧めする理由を説明します。

　英語の読解が、いわゆる4技能の基本にあることを、多くの専門家が指摘しています。英語力を向上させるのに大量の英語のインプットが必要なことは明らかで、そのために最も簡単にアクセスできるリソースは文字媒体です。また、通り過ぎてしまう会話や映画と違って、文字で書かれたテクストは、あくまで学習者のペースで読み進めていくことができます。

　その際、ポイントとなるのは、ある程度の量をまとめて読むことです（そこで、上記の1です）。以前に比べると最近は減りましたが、みなさんのなかにも、「教科書の和訳を全部書かないとわかった気がしない」という人がいるかもしれませんね。この習慣からは脱却しましょう。全文の和訳を書くというのは、時間がかかる割に英語を読む力は身につきません。一方で、よくわからないところを取り出して、文法に注意しながら丁寧に読んでみることは重要です。その場合は、和訳という作業も必要になってくるでしょう。

次に、英語で文学作品を読むことのメリットは、思い切って単純化して言えば、「言葉の使いかた」を学べるということです。みなさんが将来必要とする「高度な英語力」とは、お天気の挨拶や買い物のしかたのことではありません。本当の英語力というのは、英語で難しい交渉を進めたり、自他の意見を交換したりすることであり、そこには、人を傷つけるような皮肉や遠回しな表現もあれば、人の心をなごませるユーモアに富んだ表現も、人の心を打ち、人を動かすような表現もあります。文学作品には、こういう表現がたくさん使われています。それらを学んで身につけることが、本当に「使える」英語力の養成につながります（そこで、上記の2が重要です）。

　さらに、この小説の場合は、1990年代から2000年代初頭のアメリカの文化や社会、政治についての言及が数多く含まれています。言うまでもなく、文学作品はそれが書かれた文化や社会の産物です。ある社会に書かれた作品は、その社会に存在しているほかのさまざまなテクスト（文学作品だけでなく、映画、音楽、漫画などを含む）と相互に影響しあって、その社会の「文化」を形成します。作品をそれが書かれた時代の文脈に置いて読むと、その文化や社会についての理解が深められるので、文学作品はその地域の文化を研究することとも密接に関わります。これが、3が重要な理由です。

　そして最後に、文学作品を読むことは、自分の意見を形成する訓練をするうえでも大きな力を発揮します。みなさんは、ほかの科目でも、「大学では感想ではなく意見を書きなさい」などと言われることがあるでしょう。小説に関して意見を述べるというのは、「直前に『○○』という表現があるから、この台詞にはこういう真意がある」とか、「ここで言及されている政治家はこういう人だから、それを支持する人には××な政治的傾向がある」など、文中の特定の部分、あるいは作品の背景となっている歴史的な事実にしっかりとした根拠を見つけ、それに基づいて自分の考えを人にわかるように示すことです。そして、そういう意見は、人と議論することを通じて、お互いに確かめ合うことができます。「学問的な議論」とはそうして深めていくものです。そのために文学作品は格好の材料を提供してくれます（これが、4が重要である理由です）。

■ここからスタートです

　以上、この本のご紹介、勉強のしかた、そして、身につけることができるはずの力についてお話ししました。あとは「実行あるのみ」です。この教科書は、みなさんが興味をもって英語の学習に取り組めるように考えて作りました。楽しみながら英語力の向上を図っていただければ、編者一同、望外の喜びです。

編者代表／佐藤和哉（日本女子大学）

編　　集／日本英文学会関東支部
　　　　　奥聡一郎（関東学院大学）
　　　　　久世恭子（東洋大学）
　　　　　笹川　渉（青山学院大学）
　　　　　佐藤和哉（日本女子大学）
　　　　　古屋耕平（青山学院大学）

ワンランク上の小説の読みかた

「はしがき」で、この小説を使った「英語の勉強のしかた」について触れましたので、ここでは、どういう視点から小説に取り組めばよいか、いくつかヒントを示してみます。

小学校から高校までの国語の授業で小説を読むときには、登場人物の心情を考えたり、その小説を通じて作者の言いたいことを探ったりする作業を行うことが多かったでしょう。その結果、こういう読みかたが多くの人に馴染みが深いものとなっているかもしれませんが、それだけが小説の読みかたではありません。

たとえば、「表現に着目する」といった読みかたがあります。Chapter 1の冒頭部分に、"a clump of dark gray clouds hung in the air like an enormous cartoon thought bubble, like they were all sharing one stormy idea." (p. 6)という表現があります。これは、天気が崩れかかって雲が出てきているのを、考えている中身を表すマンガの吹き出しみたいだ、と喩えています。この比喩を読んでどういう光景が頭に浮かびますか？　このように、この小説には、巧みな比喩がたくさん使われています。そこに着目して、それらの比喩が読者にどのような印象を与えるか、を考えてみるのは、文学作品への有効なアプローチの一つです。

そのほかには、「語り手に着目する」という着眼点も有効です。この連作の小説は、いずれも「ぼく」という語り手の一人称で語られていますが、10歳の「ぼく」と中学生の「ぼく」、20歳を過ぎた「ぼく」は、当然、それぞれ、周囲の人びと――たとえば兄――に対する理解力も、自分自身についての考えかたも異なります。その違いを丁寧に読み取ってみると、面白い発見があるかもしれません。

小説などの文学作品を読んで、感想文を書いたり感想を話し合ったりするのは、とくに英語でそれを行う場合には一定の効果があります。しかし、ワンランク上のアウトプットを目指すならば、上で述べたような読みかたをしたあと、それにもとづいて、作品の「良いところ」を人に伝える文章を書いてみることをお勧めします。「私」を主語にして、その物語のどこが好きなのかを述べるだけではなく、「この物語」を主語にして、その物語のどういう点が効果的だったり印象的だったりするのかを客観的に書くことに挑戦してみてください。「書く」ことで、「読む」活動が完結します。ここまでできれば、立派に「ワンランク上の小説の読みかた」だと言えるでしょう。

（佐藤 和哉）

Contents •

Michael Larson

NOTES ON BROTHERHOOD

English Literature in the Classroom Vol. 1

For my brothers, Rob and Chris and Danny

And, as always, for J

Chapter 1

Let Us Go Out Into the Field

This is a story of two brothers, which, as the title alludes to, is a story as old as time or at least as old as history. However, I hope the piece's specificity removes it from the realm of archetype and captures something of what it was like to grow up in the mid-1990s in America. Although the Cold War was over, for many people the military continued to play a significant role in everyday life, especially families with members serving in the armed forces and those near the sprawling bases, like Ft. Lewis in Washington State. In movies and TV shows, video games and popular songs, the military was woven into the culture.

In addition to the focus on the two brothers, this story is also about the stage in life when one begins to leave childhood behind and peer into the world of adults. For the protagonist, this takes the form of understanding what his older brother already knows about their family. In that way, it is a typical story of discovery.

これからみなさんが読むのは、聖書から借りたタイトルが暗示するとおり、ふたりの兄弟についての物語であり、昔からよくある、あるいは少なくとも人類の歴史が始まってから見られるお話です。ですが、これは人類の原型として描かれる兄弟の話ではなく、1990年代半ばのアメリカで育つことがどのようなものであったかを、本作中の具体的な描写によってとらえることができればと思います。東西冷戦は終わりましたが、多くの人々にとって、軍隊は日常生活の中で重要な役割を担い続けていました。軍隊に所属する家族がいる家庭、ワシントン州のフォート・ルイスのように広大な基地の近くで暮らしている家庭にとっては特にそうでした。映画やテレビ番組、テレビゲーム、ポピュラー音楽では、軍隊は文化の中に織り込まれていました。

Chapter 1 では、「ぼく（ダン）」とその兄ロブのふたりの兄弟に焦点を当てることに加え、子ども時代を離れて大人の世界をのぞき見始める人生の段階も描いています。主人公の「ぼく」にとっては、自分たちの家族について兄がすでに知っていることを理解するという形式をとっており、その意味で、典型的な発見の物語となっています。

第1部はリトルリーグの野球の試合の場面から始まります。主人公の日常の描写から、「ぼく（ダン）」と、兄のロブ、兄の友人レニー、父や母との関わりを読み取りましょう。

Pre-reading

1. ワシントン州とはどのような場所なのか、調べてみましょう。

2. 次に示す、野球に使われる英語やルールについて調べてみましょう。

[batter, pitcher, outfielders, inning, dugout, grounders, infielders, shortstop]

Vocabulary

次の語の定義を下記のａからｊの中から選びなさい。

1. lean	**2.** chant	**3.** squint	**4.** knee	**5.** glisten
6. bruise	**7.** ignore	**8.** glow	**9.** resentment	**10.** concentrate

a.　the joint that bends in the middle of your leg

b.　to behave as if you had not heard or seen someone or something

c.　to move or bend your body in a particular direction

d.　a steady radience or light or a strong feeling of pleasure etc.

e.　to shine and look wet or oily

f.　to think very carefully about something that you are doing

g.　to repeat a word or phrase again and again

h.　a feeling of anger because something has happened that you think is unfair

i.　a purple or brown mark on your skin that you get because you have fallen, been hit etc.

j.　to look at something with your eyes partly closed in order to see better

(3) I watched Rob standing with one foot in the batter's box and one foot out. The **head** of his bat rested on the dirt and the **handle** was balanced against his thigh, while he pulled the straps of his hitting gloves tight. Above the opposing team's outfielders, **a clump of** dark gray clouds hung in the air like an enormous **cartoon thought** 5 **bubble**, like they were all sharing one stormy idea.

Two outs in **the bottom of the sixth**, the last inning according to the Little League rulebook. **Our team was down by one**, runners on first and second, the count was **three balls to one strike**. I leaned against the fence in front of the home dugout, **my fingers looped through the** 10 **chain links**. My dad was coaching because our regular coach Mr. Miller had been called on to help **put out** a blaze in the woods behind the high school with his volunteer firefighting unit; Dad sometimes **helped out with** our team, **hitting grounders to the infielders during practice**, and he was the closest thing we had to an assistant coach. 15

(4) The opposing pitcher had thrown the whole game and looked **dog tired**. This inning, **he'd struck out the eight and nine-hole hitters**, and then lost his feel for the strike zone and gave up two **walks**. Dad was going through the signs, and he put up four fingers which meant **take the next pitch**. 20

Rob **shook his head** ever so slightly before stepping back into the box and **coiling** into his batting stance. "Good eye, now, good eye," I chanted, but I just knew he was going to swing.

The outfielders squinted in toward home plate, and the runner on first took a step off **the bag**; Lenny, the runner on second, **measured** 25 **out** his own lead, looking over one shoulder then the other, **like a thief** who knows he's being watched. The shortstop had taken a knee on the infield dirt **between pitches**, but now he got to his feet, **scuffed the ground with one of his cleats**, pounded a fist into his glove.

The pitcher's forearm glistened with sweat. His throwing hand was 30 hidden inside his glove where it gripped the ball. He raised his leg, twisting through his **windup**, then strode forward, his arms flying apart.

Title　Let Us Go Into the Field: field は「(冒頭の場面で描かれる)野球場」、「(Unit 4の軍事演習がおこなわれる)野原」などUnit 1-4で描かれる物語の舞台を表している。タイトルは旧約聖書『創世記』に登場するカインが、弟のアベルを誘い出す時に述べる言葉である(4章8節)。その後、アベルはカインを殺すというエピソードが語られる。ここでは、「野球をしに行こう」という意味とともに、語り手の「ぼく(ダン)」と兄(ロブ)の不和が示唆される。

2　head: (バットのボールを打つ方の)先端部分。通例endという。

　　handle: (バットの握る部分も含めた)柄の部分。

4-5　a clump of:「ひとかたまりの」

5-6　cartoon thought bubble: マンガなどに使われる、登場人物が考えていることを書き込む雲形の枠。

7　the bottom of the sixth:「6回裏」

8-9　Our team was ... : この1文は接続詞がなくコンマ(,)のみで節・句・節が並列されている。

8　down by one:「1点差で負けている」

9　three balls to one strike: 一般にバットを振るには絶好のカウントとされる。

10-11　my fingers (being) looped through the chain links:「指を金網にひっかけた」 主節の主語 I と異なる独立分詞構文で、my fingersを主語にし、鎖状になっている金網をつかんでいる様子。

12　put out:「消火する」

13-14　help out with:「(困った時に)手助けする」

14　hitting grounders to the infielders during practice:「練習のときに内野手にノックでゴロを打って」

16-17　dog tired: = dog-tired「ひどく疲れ果てて」

17　he'd struck out the eight and nine-hole hitters:「8番打者と9番打者を三振に仕留めて」

18　walks:「フォアボール」

19-20　take the next pitch:「次の球を見送れということ」

21　shook his head:

　　Q. 1 ロブはサインに対してどのように返答したでしょう。

　　　1. したがうと合図した。　　**2.** 拒否した。

22　coiling:「身体を丸めて」

25　the bag:「ベース」

25-26　measured out:「距離を測った」

26　**Q. 2** なぜ like a thief という比喩が使われているのでしょうか。

28　between pitches:「投球の間に」

28-29　scuffed the ground with one of his cleats:「片方のスパイクで地面を蹴った」

32　windup: ピッチャーが両手を頭上に上げて投球動作に入ること。

Unit : 1

(5) *Hit, hit, hit,* I hoped with one half of my mind. *Out, out, out,* I pleaded with the other.

A hit because Lenny would race home and **tie the game**—the 35 rulebook said **no extra innings**, so a hit meant we couldn't lose and might even win **if we pushed across another run**. Dad wouldn't be happy to have his sign **brushed off**, but **he'd** get over it. A hit would mean **no sulking** on the drive home and might even mean **TacoTime** for dinner. A hit would mean **we'd be happy together again**. 40

An out would be game over, no need for pride or celebration. **No listening to Rob talk** for the next month about his game-tying hit with two out in the last inning. An out would show him, teach him **a lesson**. You need to listen sometimes, stop **testing the limits**.

If this sounds strange to you, if this contest between hope and 45 dread **rings unfamiliar**, if in your mind the difference between love and hate is a clear bright line, **not a hair to one side or the other**, then maybe you never had a brother.

(6) On the ride home, the van was quiet. Dad drove, I was in the passenger 50 seat, and Rob was in the backseat next to Lenny, who in addition to being our team's third baseman and my brother's best friend, was Mr. Miller's son. His mom had dropped him off at our farm before the game and my dad said he could ride back with us, and she could pick him up whenever was good for her. 55

"**Man**, what a game," Lenny said, as we merged onto the **freeway**. "**So close**."

I liked Lenny for the most part, but sometimes he involved himself in my brother's stupid ideas, like when he and Rob said they'd teach me to snowboard and brought me up three chair lifts to the top of 60 **White Pass Mountain**, then took off—Rob saying, "Bye, **loser**," over his shoulder as he **sped** away. By the time I reached the bottom of the second lift, **I'd fallen so many times I could feel bruises** forming on my arms and legs and **my ribs hurt so bad I was in tears**. I asked the

35 A hit because: = I hoped for a hit because

tie the game:「試合を同点にする」　*Cf.* his game-tying hit（42行目）

36 no extra innings:「延長戦はない」

37 if we pushed across another run:「さらに1点をいれれば」

38 brushed off:「無視される」

he'd: = he would

39 no sulking:「父もロブも不機嫌になることはない」

TacoTime: メキシコ料理を提供するファーストフードのチェーン店。

40 we'd be happy together again:

Q. 3 ▷ これはどのようなことを言っているのでしょう。

41-42 No listening to Rob talk: = There is no need to listen to Rob talk

43 a lesson: 続く1文がその教訓の内容。

44 testing the limits:「限界ぎりぎりのことを試すこと」

46 ring unfamiliar:「聞いてもぴんとこない」

47 not a hair to one side or the other:「どちらの側にも髪の毛1本ずれる余地もないほどに」 *Cf.* a hair:「ほんのわずかな量も」

56 Man:「なんてこった」

freeway:「高速道路」

57 So close:「接戦だった」

61 White Pass Mountain: 物語の舞台であるワシントン州にある、スキー場で有名な山。1990年代半ば、スノーボードが流行した。

loser: 相手をけなして「意気地なし」

62 sped: speedの過去形。

63 I'd fallen so many times I could feel bruises:

Q. 4 ▷ = I (　　　　) fallen so many times (　　　　　　) I could feel bruises

64 my ribs hurt so bad I was in tears:

Q. 5 ▷ = my ribs hurt so bad (　　　　) I was in tears.

attendant **if I could take a chair down**, and on my way to the bottom ₆₅ I passed the two of them coming up on the same lift; my face was red from crying, and I looked away as they **whooped** and clapped at me. I went into the lodge and found my mom, who'd driven us up in her truck, and told her what had happened. When Lenny and Rob came in for lunch, she grabbed her keys from her purse and **drug** Rob out ₇₀ to the icy parking lot; we drove home, skipping the afternoon, though we'd bought full-day passes. They kept calling me a **tattletale**, but I ignored them.

(7)   This had been a few months ago, and since then Mr. Miller let me join the baseball team despite my being younger than all the other ₇₅ boys, who were in Rob's grade. The glow of my gratitude toward our coach extended to Lenny and helped me forget the bit of resentment I continued to hold against him. Still, as we drove home, **I couldn't help but suspect he was getting my brother going on purpose**.

"One run. We needed one run." Rob slapped his glove against his ₈₀ knee. "**God damn**."

"No, no, no," Dad said, looking in the rearview mirror. "That's a no on the language."

"**Sorry, we did**."

He'd hit **a line drive, a screamer** curving toward left field, but at ₈₅ the last second the shortstop had leaped up, **his legs bicycling in the air**, and snagged the ball in the top of his glove. **A snow cone catch**. Three outs, **ballgame**.

"You need to pay attention when I'm giving signs." It started to **drizzle**, and Dad switched on the windshield wipers. "Didn't you see ₉₀ me give **the take sign**?"

"I was concentrating on hitting." From the sound of his voice, I could tell Rob was looking out the window at the green-grey farmland and passing traffic.

"**You swung at ball four**." ₉₅

Had Dad not seen my brother **shake him off?** Or was he just

65 if I could take a chair down:「(滑って降りるのではなく)リフトに座って降りられるかどうか」

67 whooped:「叫んで囃し立てた」

70 drug:「引っ張った」 一般的にdragの過去形はdraggedだが、アメリカの口語表現ではdrugの形も用いられる。

72 tattletale:「ちくり屋」

78-79 couldn't help but suspect:「疑わざるを得なかった」

79 he was getting my brother going on purpose:「レニーは兄をそそのかしていた」

81 God damn:「ちくしょう」 不快感、失望、怒り、いらだち、あるいは驚きなどを強調する口語表現。直訳すると「神が呪いますように」。このように主に口語で用いられる冒涜的な罵りの言葉をswear wordという。

84 Sorry, we did:

Q.6 = We're sorry that we used the words "(   )(   )".

85-88 試合の回想。89行目から再び車内の場面に変わる。

85 a line drive, a screamer:「ライナー」 ノーバウンドで鋭く飛んでいく打球。

86-87 his legs bicycling in the air:「ショートの足が宙を漕いで」

87 A snow cone catch:「かき氷式キャッチ」 ボールがかき氷のようにグローブの先端からはみ出ている捕球。

88 ballgame: = ball game「試合終了」

90 drizzle:「霧雨が降る」

91 the take sign:「ボールを見送れのサイン」 19-20行目以下を参照。

95 You swung at ball four: ボール球だったので、バットを振らなければフォアボールを選ぶことができたことを言っている。

96 shake him off:「父のサインを拒否する」

pretending not to have **noticed**? Things had been tense between him and Rob for weeks. **Maybe he was trying to let this one go**.

My brother said, "I wanted to **get it over with**."

"Well, you did. Not the way you ought to have **though**. You need ₁₀₀ to be patient. Use your head. **Take the pitch and we have a runner on third**."

I heard my brother whisper to Lenny, "Ask him."

"Hey, Mr. Overton, **can Rob come over to my house?** My mom can take both of us to school tomorrow morning." ₁₀₅

"**School night**," I muttered.

"Shut up," Rob hissed behind me.

He must've known what the answer was going to be, which was why he'd gotten Lenny to ask. I didn't understand the reason, but for the last couple of weeks, my brother had put on an **attitude** when he ₁₁₀ talked to our parents.

97 noticed: = noticed that Rob ignored Dad's sign

98 Maybe he was trying to let this one go:「たぶん、父はこの一件をなかったことにしようとしていたのだろう」

99 get it over with:「いやなこと（ここでは試合）を終わらせる」

100 though:「けれども」副詞として文末で用いる。

101-102 Take the pitch and we have a runner on third:「ボールを見送れば3塁に走者を進められる」 3ボール1ストライクでピッチャーが投げたボールがおそらくボール球だったので、見送ればロブがフォアボールとなり、満塁にすることができたと言っている。

104 can Rob come over to my house?: アメリカでは、小学生くらいになると親しい友達の家に泊まりに行くこと（sleepover）がよくある。

106 school night: 学校がある前日の夜。

110 attitude:「生意気な態度、反抗的な態度」

💬 **Expression**　　本文を参考に次の表現を英語になおす時に空所に入る語を書きなさい。

1. 私は彼女が丘の上に立っているのを見ていた。

I watched her (　　　　　　　) on the hill.

2. その少年は先生の前で行儀よくふるまった。

The boy behaved himself in (　　　　　　　) of his teacher.

3. 私は彼のことを笑わずにはいられなかった。

I couldn't help (　　　　　　　) laugh at her.

4. 君はもっと注意を払うべきだ。

You should (　　　　　　　) more attention.

5. 彼は積極的な姿勢をとるふりをしている。

He (　　　　　　　) on positive attitude.

💡 **Comprehension**　　次の問いに答えなさい。

1. その日になぜ語り手とロブの父親が野球のコーチをしていたのでしたか。

2. he'd get over it. (ℓ.38) とありますが、なぜですか。

3. A hit would mean we'd be happy together again. (ℓ.40) のwouldの意味はなんですか。

4. then maybe you never had a brother. (ℓℓ.47-48) から兄弟がいると何がわかるのですか。

5. On the ride home, the van was quiet. (ℓ.50) この状況から何がわかりますか。

6. but sometimes he involved himself in my brother's stupid ideas, (ℓℓ.58-59) の例を説明しなさい。

7. They kept calling me a tattletale, (ℓ.72) とありますが、なぜこのようなことを言ったのですか。

_____

8. Rob slapped his glove against his knee. (ℓℓ.80-81) とありますが、この時のロブの気持ちを説明しなさい。

_____

9. Things had been tense between him and Rob for weeks. (ℓℓ.97-98) の過去完了にはどのような意味があると思われますか。

_____

10. He must've known what the answer was going to be, which was why he'd gotten Lenny to ask. (ℓℓ.108-109) ロブはどんな答えが返ってくると予想したのでしょうか。

_____

⇄ Discussion

1. "like they were all sharing one stormy idea" (ℓ.6) の "one stormy idea" からどのような印象を受けますか、話し合ってみましょう。

_____

2. "_Hit, hit, hit,_ I hoped with one half of my mind. _Out, out, out,_ I pleaded with the other." (ℓℓ.33-34) の箇所について、主人公はなぜこのように考えるのか、話し合ってみましょう。

_____

✎ Writing

Choose a member of your family. Describe him or her and write about the relationship between that person and you.

_____

_____

_____

_____

_____

_____

_____

_____

Grammar Guide — 分詞構文の意味

He raised his leg, twisting through his windup, then strode forward, his arms flying apart.(ℓℓ.31-32)では分詞構文が効果的に用いられています。「彼は足を上げ、(と同時に) 投球前のワインドアップで体をひねらせ、それから足を前に出し、(その結果として) 彼の両腕が別々の方向に動いていくという」、ピッチャーの球を投げる様子がスローモーションのように展開されています。

分詞構文の動作主が主語と異なるときには分詞の前に意味上の主語を置きます。his arms は主語のHe と異なるために分詞 flyingの前に置かれている意味上の主語です。分詞構文の取る意味は上記の例での付帯状況や結果の他にも時や条件などがあります、このような分詞構文によって、読み手は前後の文脈から重層的な意味を推し量ります。

Unit : 2

このUnitでは、主人公のぼく（ダン）と家族が住んでいる地域の様子が明らかになってきます。日本とは異なる状況もあるようです。

Pre-reading

1. この場合のthe reservationとはどのような場所でしょうか。本文の内容を参考に調べてみましょう。

2. Veteranとはどういう人を指すのか、調べてみましょう。

Vocabulary

次の語の定義を下記のaからjの中から選びなさい。

1. sigh	**2.** mope	**3.** pasture	**4.** smear	**5.** property
6. egg...on	**7.** arc	**8.** crack	**9.** lope	**10.** smack

a. to spread a liquid or soft substance over a surface, especially in a careless or untidy way

b. to break or to make something break, either so that it gets lines on its surface, or so that it breaks into pieces

c. to spend your time doing nothing and feeling sorry for yourself

d. to hit something hard against something else so that it makes a short loud noise

e. to encourage someone to do something, especially something that they do not want to do or should not do

f. a land or a field that is covered with grass and is used for cattle, sheep etc to feed on

g. to make a curved shape or line

h. to run easily with long steps

i. to breathe in and out making a long sound, especially because you are bored, disappointed, tired etc.

j. a building, a piece of land, or both together

(8) **D**ad shook his head. "Sorry, Lenny, he needs to get his grades up before he can be **staying over** anywhere on a school night."

Rob sighed, and for a while, we rode in silence. Dad had gotten off the freeway and we were about ten minutes from home, passing through 5 the **reservation**—the vast tract of prairie and forest land that belonged to the military, where **the Army**'s soldiers played **war games**—when Rob pointed out the window, telling Lenny to look, look.

Since the morning, when **we'd** driven past this area, they'd put up a big wooden **roadblock** on the dirt track that led onto the **Res'**. It stood 10 there like a section of detached fence but with white and **safety-orange** stripes and a sign in the middle, which **read *Exercises in Progress*.**

"This has to be—" Rob said, "It's the same as last year. **Tactical training**."

"Oh, the **paratroopers**," Lenny said. 15

(9) Rob must have told him about the **Special Forces platoon**, which had been blown off their landing area and accidentally parachuted onto our farm. We eventually **got the commanding officer to** show us his knife, with its long, **serrated** edge and a compass embedded in the handle. 20

"Weren't you in the Army, Mr. Overton?" Lenny asked.

Rob said, "Yeah, but he was a lawyer. Like for soldiers who get arrested."

Dad had retired from the military and spent the past couple years **setting up a real estate practice**. Our mom had also been in the military, 25 and she and Dad had met on **base** in **Colorado**, before moving out to the West Coast. She still worked as a nurse in the **veteran's hospital**.

Dad said, "I wasn't always a lawyer. I started in the **infantry**, was in **Airborne**, I did **all that stuff**."

"Yeah, a long time ago." 30

Out of the corner of my eye, I saw Dad **wince** and **flick a glance** in the rearview mirror.

2   staying over: 他の人の家で一夜を過ごすこと。

6   reservation:「軍用地」

7   the Army: = the Army of the United States「合衆国陸軍」

    war games:（複数形で）「軍事演習」

9   we'd: = we had

10   roadblock:「バリケード」

    Res':= reservation（6行目の注を参照）

11   safety-orange: 注意喚起のために使われる色鮮やかなオレンジ色。

12   read:「～と書かれていた」

    Exercises in Progress:「軍事演習中」

13-14 Tactical training:「戦術訓練」

15   paratroopers:「パラシュート部隊」

16   Special Forces platoon:「特殊部隊の小隊」

18   got the commanding officer to :「部隊長に～してもらった」

19   serrated:「のこぎり状の」

25   setting up a real estate practice:「不動産業をおこなう」

26   base:「基地」

    Colorado:「コロラド州」アメリカ西部に位置する。

27   veteran's hospital:「退役軍人向けの病院」

28   infantry:「歩兵部隊」

29   Airborne:「空挺部隊」

    all that stuff:「あれこれ」ここでは軍事演習などを指す。

31   Out of the corner of my eye:「視界の端で」

    wince:「顔をしかめる」

    flick a glance:「ちらっと見る」

Unit: 2

(10)   By the time we got home, the rain had thinned so **you** hardly even noticed. Soon as Dad parked the van behind our house, Rob jumped out and grabbed his practice bat and the five-**gallon** bucket of worn 35 baseballs from the garage. Dad told him not to use those. "Use the **whiffle balls**. You can only hit those so far. We've already lost half the balls to your homerun practice."

"Yeah," Rob moped, putting the bucket back and **making like** he was going to get the whiffles. 40

But after Dad went in the house, Rob went back into the garage and grabbed the regular baseballs anyway. I knew he was looking for an excuse to stay outside, so he could listen for helicopters or a troop transport plane. The afternoon shadows were stretching toward evening, and a chill blew through the trees. **I had half a mind to** go into 45 my room and read *Hatchet*, but I stayed outside with them. **Truth was**, I wanted to see the army men, too.

(11)   A year ago, we'd been playing **SNES** in the living room when we heard a sound like thunder and rushed outside to see a **C-130** flying low over the trees behind our property. Little dots dropped **out** the 50 back of the plane, unfolding into green umbrella shapes as the soldiers' parachutes opened and they floated down like seeds blown off a dandelion. My mom was in the barn, and my brother and I rushed out to her. The soldiers had landed in our rear pastures and were packing up their parachutes. A few stared at my mom's **Quarter Horses like** 55 they'd never seen such large animals.

(12)   One man had seen us and walked over, **slinging** his rifle to the side. Beneath his helmet, his forehead and cheeks were **smeared with green-and-black face paint**; he smiled and raised a hand to us from the other side of the fence. Ignoring the gray mare sniffing at his shoulder, 60 he explained to my mom that his platoon was on a weekend-long tactical training exercise. They hadn't expected to land there, but, in any case, part of their mission involved establishing relations with any

33　you: 人一般を指す総称の you。

35　gallon: アメリカでは約3.79リットル。なお、イギリスでは約4.55リットル。

37　whiffle balls: 穴の空いたプラスチック製のあまり飛ばない練習用ボール。

39　making like: 「〜なそぶりを見せて」

45　I had half a mind to: 「〜したい気持ちもあった」

46　*Hatchet*: ゲイリー・ポールセン (Gary Paulsen, 1939-2021) による、1986年に出版された少年向けの小説。主人公ブライアンは、カナダの森に不時着し、過酷な環境の中でたくましくサバイバル生活を送る。アメリカで出版時から現在まで広く読まれている。

　　Truth was: = The truth was that

48　ここから74行目まで前の年の回想が語られる。

48　SNES: 日本ではスーパーファミコンの名称で知られる、1990年に任天堂が発売して大ヒットした家庭用ゲーム機。アメリカではこの名称で知られる。Super Nintendo Entertainment System の略。

49　C-130: アメリカのロッキード社製の巨大な戦術輸送機。現在でも製造されている。

50　out: = out of

55　Quarter Horses: 「クォーターホース」アメリカで改良された、筋肉質でがっしりとした体型の馬の品種。400メートル (1マイル約1,600mの4分の1〈=クォーターマイル〉) を速く走ることからこの名前がつけられた。

　　like: 口語でas ifと同じように使われる。

57　slinging: 「吊り下げて」

58-59　smeared with green-and-black face paint: 「緑と黒のフェイスペイントで塗られた」軍事演習のために迷彩色を塗っている。

Unit: 2

civilians they met, and he asked if **they might camp for the night on** 65 **our property**. Rob tugged on our mom's sleeve, **both of us whispering** that she absolutely had to let them stay.

For two boys who'd grown up watching *G.I. Joe: A Real American Hero* and shopping for **camping gear** at the **army surplus store** in town, **hardly anything could've been more impressive than a camo-smeared** 70 **officer** waltzing toward us in full gear, **an M-16 dangling from one shoulder**. Mom offered the lieutenant and his men a spot near the front of our property. In an odd, **toothy** sort of way, the soldier said, "Thanks to you, **ma'am**."

(13)   Wondering if the soldiers would come back this year, we **kept** 75 **stealing glances** at the grey-blue sky above the trees, **our ears pricked for** the far-off music of a plane engine. In an empty pasture, which Mom had **cleared** of horses to regrow the grass, we established a **diamond** with a moss-covered rock for first base, fallen branches for second and third, and my brother's hat for home plate. He made me 80 play outfield while **Lenny tossed him batting practice,** the rule being he only got to circle the bases if he hit one over my head. Like with our Little League team, where Mr. Miller usually only put me in as a **pinch runner** toward the end of **lopsided** games, I was happy just **shagging flies** and moving around outside.   85

Rob hit a few hard foul balls and two **line drives** got past Lenny, but **nothing so far** I couldn't track it down. When the two of them switched places, I heard Rob say, "No way you'll **crack** one all the way out past **him**."

(14)   I hadn't realized how far back I was and started to walk toward 90 the infield. Lenny kept hitting grounders and nothing made it past my brother. Rob egged him on, saying, "C'mon, this is embarrassing. **What've you got noodle arms?**"

I'd crept in nearly to the branch we were using for second base, when Rob said he was going to throw his **heater**. He **delivered**, and 95 Lenny **connected with** the pitch **so hard** the bat sung like a golf club.

65-66 they might camp for the night on our property: 演習中の軍隊が個人所有の敷地を借りて野営することは珍しいことではなかった。

66 both of us whispering: = and both of us whispered

68-69 *G.I. Joe: A Real American Hero*: 1983年9月12日から1986年11月20日と1989年9月2日から1992年1月20日までアメリカで放映されたテレビアニメ。アメリカ軍の特殊部隊を率いるG.I. ジョーが、世界征服をもくろむ組織「コブラ」と戦う物語。フィギュアも発売され大人気となった。

69 camping gear: 「キャンプ用品」

army surplus store: 「軍払い下げ品の販売店」

70 hardly anything could've been more impressive than ... : 「〜より印象的なものはおよそ考えられなかっただろう」

70-71 a camo-smeared officer: = an officer smeared with camouflage paint. 57行目から登場する迷彩色を顔に塗った軍人。

71-72 an M-16 dangling from one shoulder: = with an M-16 dangling from one shoulder.

73 toothy: 「歯を見せて」

74 ma'am: = madam. 敬意を払った丁寧な言い方。

ここまでで回想が終わり、次の段落から47行目までの話に戻る。

75-76 kept stealing glances: 「何度もちらちらと視線を送り続けた」

76-77 our ears pricked for: = with our ears pricked for 「〜に耳を澄ませながら」

78 cleared: clear A of B. 「AからBを取りのぞいた」ここでAにあたるのは関係代名詞の先行詞 empty pasture。

79 diamond: 「内野」

81 Lenny tossed him batting practice: 「レニーがボールをトスして、ロブは打撃練習をした」

83-84 pinch runner: 「代走」

84 lopsided: 「点差がついて一方的な」   shagging flies: 「フライを捕球する」

86 line drives: Unit 1, 85行目を参照。

87 nothing so far: = Rob hit nothing so far that

88 crack: 「かっ飛ばす」

89 **Q.1** 〉〉 himは誰でしょう？

93 What've you got, noodle arms?: 「何ができるんだ、そのへなちょこ腕で」

94 I'd: = I had

95 heater: 「速球」   delivered: = pitched 「ボールを投げた」

connected with: (口語)「うまい具合にあわせた」

96 so hard: = so hard that

The ball flew far above my head, arcing across the sky, and fell toward the trees. A branch cracked as it landed somewhere out past the fence, in the woods which **weren't** even on our property **but** part of the military reservation.   100

Lenny jogged to first, his finger in the air, saying, "Homerun! Homerun! That's how you end a game." He kicked the first-base rock as he passed it, still celebrating. It reminded me of how his voice had sounded on the mountain, **when he and Rob passed by on the chair lift, their laughter echoing off the trees**. The second-base branch snapped 105 when he stepped on it, and I was just a few feet from him now. I held out my hand for a **high five**, and he loped toward me, **winding up to smack my palm as hard as he could**.

99 weren't: ... but ... : not A but B「AでなくB」

104-105 when he and Rob passed by on the chair lift, their laughter echoing off the trees: Unit 1, 58行目以下を参照。their laughter以下は独立分詞構文。

107 high five:「ハイタッチ」

108 **Q. 2** "winding up to smack my palm as hard as he could" はどのような動作をしているか実際におこなってみましょう。

💬 Expression 本文を参考に次の表現を英語に直す時に空所に入る語を書きなさい。

1. しばらくは何も見えなかった。

For a (　　　　　　　　), we could scarcely see anything.

2. 彼の夢は会社を起こすことだった。

His dream was to (　　　　　　) up his company.

3. ちょっと手を貸していただければと思っていたのですが。

I was wondering (　　　　　　) you could help me.

4. 兄が私を外で遊ばせた。

My brother (　　　　　　) me play outfield.

5. その出来事が彼の声が山でどのように響いたかを私に思い出させた。

That accident reminded me (　　　　　　) how his voice had sounded on the mountain.

💡 Comprehension 次の問いに答えなさい。

1. *Exercises in Progress* (ℓ.12) の標識はどのようなもので、意味は何でしょうか。

2. 「ぼく(ダン)」の父は軍隊でどのような仕事をしていましたか。

3. I saw Dad wince and flick a glance in the rearview mirror. (ℓℓ.31-32) には、父のどのような気持ちが現れているでしょうか。

4. he was looking for an excuse to stay outside, (ℓℓ.42-43) は、どうして言い訳を探していたのですか。

5. The afternoon shadows were stretching toward evening, and a chill blew through the trees. (ℓℓ.44-45) とは、どのような状況ですか。

6. Ignoring the gray mare sniffing at his shoulder, (ℓ.60) の分詞構文を訳し、兵士が母に説明したことをまとめなさい。

_____

7. the rule being he only got to circle the bases if he hit one over my head. (ℓℓ.81-82) の being に気をつけて、どのようなことなのか説明しなさい。

_____

8. "No way you'll crack one all the way out past him." (ℓℓ.88-89) には、ロブのどのような気持ちが込められているでしょうか。

_____

9. I hadn't realized how far back I was and started to walk toward the infield. (ℓℓ.90-91) とは、どのようなことを指しているのでしょうか。

_____

10. レニーが最後に球を打った様子を簡単にまとめなさい。

_____

Unit : 2

⇄ **Discussion**

1. 1990年代半ばのアメリカの家庭にあったSNESや _G.I. Joe_ などの子供をめぐる文化について日本と比較しながら話し合ってみましょう。

2. 兄弟にとって、兵士たちの存在はどのようなものだったでしょうか、本文からそれがわかる箇所を示しながら、話し合ってみましょう。

✎ Writing

What kind of books did you read in your childhood?

_____

_____

_____

_____

_____

_____

_____

_____

_____

_____

_____

Grammar Guide ── 過去完了　過去より以前の出来事を指します。

　By the time we got home, the rain had thinned.(ℓ.33)では家に着いた時点より以前に雨が小降りになってきたこと指すために、過去完了の時制を用いています。物語では過去時制で語られるのが基本ですが、過去完了が用いられているときは物語の中で進行している事柄よりもさらに過去のことを描写していることに気をつけましょう。

Unit: 3

「ぼく（ダン）」と兄のロブ、ロブと父、父と母など、家族の中でのそれぞれの微妙な人間関係が描かれています。言動から読み取りましょう。

📖 Pre-reading

1. the Cold War について調べてみましょう。

2. （携帯）電話の歴史についてまとめてみましょう。

🎙 Vocabulary

次の語の定義を下記の a から j の中から選びなさい。

1. sting	**2.** fling	**3.** trip	**4.** stomp	**5.** weird
6. malicious	**7.** stiffen	**8.** accomplish	**9.** peer	**10.** thicket

a. to catch somebody's foot and make them fall or almost fall

b. to succeed in doing something, especially after trying very hard

c. to throw or move something roughly and carelessly

d. to look very carefully at something, especially because you are having difficulty seeing it

e. very strange and unusual, and difficult to understand or explain

f. a group of bushes and small trees

g. very unkind and cruel, and deliberately behaving in a way that is likely to upset or hurt someone

h. to make something hurt with a sudden sharp pain, or to hurt like this

i. to become firm, straight, or still because you feel angry or anxious

j. to walk with heavy steps or to put your foot down very hard, especially because you are angry

(15) **A**s I felt the stinging slap of his hand against my own, I stuck out my foot and his smile froze. His foot **caught** and he went down **face first**.

Now Rob was laughing, and Lenny rolled over in the wet grass. His hand had landed in an old pile of horse **dung** and there was a red spot where he'd bit his lip when he fell. He was already pushing himself up, and I **knew better than to hang around**. I ran across the pasture toward the house. **Ducking** through the boards of the fence, I glanced back and saw Lenny two steps behind me, his hand **smeared** with green-yellow dung and his face twisted in rage. **"Get over here."**

But I was already sprinting through the yard. I was slower than him, but I only needed to **make the house**, the back door. I grabbed the knob, flung it open—**what had possessed me to trip him**? I kicked off my shoes in the **mudroom**, then something grabbed the back of my shirt. I went down among the collection of sneakers and rubber boots. Rob was behind Lenny, whose lip was starting to **swell**.

(16) He raised his foot as if to stomp me, but in the next second the door opened. Mom flung out an arm, pushing him back against the washing machine. My mom wasn't a big woman, but she **was used to handling** horses, and Lenny probably **barely** weighed a hundred **pounds**.

"What's going on?" she asked.

Rob still held a baseball, and he rubbed it against his **pant leg like an apple**, "Dan tripped him."

Mom pulled me up by the arm. "Well, this isn't how to solve things."

In the end, she made me apologize to Lenny, who stood there sucking on his **busted** lip, looking like he wanted to **knock my block off**. As I finished saying I was sorry, I heard footsteps through the house, then the door to the kitchen opened and there was Dad.

"Thought I told you not to use **those balls**," he said, staring at Rob. **"I want every single one of those picked up. Can I have a word**, Anne?"

2　caught: 自動詞で「（意図せずに何かに）ひっかかった」

3　face first:「顔から」

5　dung:「糞」

7　knew better than to hang round:「その場でぐずぐずするほどばかな真似はしなかった」

8　Ducking:「ひょいと屈んで」

9　smeared: Unit 2, 58-59行目で、回想に登場する兵士は緑と黒で迷彩色に顔を塗り、ダンの憧れの存在であったが、ここでは対照的にレニーの手が馬の糞で、緑と黄色のまだら模様になるという惨めな様子が描写されている。

10　Get over here:「（怒って）こっちに来い」

12　make the house:「家に着く」　make:「たどり着く」

13　what had possessed me to trip him?:「どうしてぼくはレニーをつまずかせようなんて思ったのだろうか」

14　mudroom: 屋内にある、汚れた靴や衣服を脱ぐ場所。

16　swell:「腫れる」

19　was used to handling :「～を扱うのに慣れていた」

20　barely:「せいぜい」

　　pounds: 1ポンドは0.4536キログラム。

22　pant leg:「ズボンの片方の足」

22-23　like an apple: リンゴを食べる前にズボンでこすることがある。

27　busted:（口語）「怪我をして切れた」

27-28　knock my block off:「ぼくの頭をぶん殴って吹っとばす」　block:（俗語）「頭」

30　Thought: = I thought (that)

Q. 1 》　those ballsとはどのボールですか？

31　I want every single one of those picked up:「ボールをひとつ残らず拾ってきなさい」
　　Can I have a word ...?:「話をいいか？」他の人に聞かれないように話したいという意味。

(17)   It was weird to hear him call Mom by her name, though all I cared about was slipping out of the mudroom and into the house, where I retreated to my room. From my window, I watched Rob and Lenny ₃₅ outside. They walked to the fence and shook hands before Lenny turned and started to head down the **driveway**. Rob went into the pasture to collect the baseballs.

The driveway took Lenny past the outside of my room, and, standing on my bed, I slid the window open and whispered at him ₄₀ through the **screen**. "Where you going? You're not going to help him?"

He looked up and saw me watching him. "**Whatever, man**. I'm out of here."

"What? You going to walk home?"

He shook his head. "Don't worry. You'll **get yours**." ₄₅

Then I noticed Mrs. Miller's car had pulled into our driveway. He **must've heard** the engine when his mom drove up the road to our farm. He got in the passenger side and started talking to her—undoubtedly telling her about my maliciousness and the **bump** on his lip, all the ways he'd been mistreated. He and Rob **would have plenty of chances** ₅₀ to **get back at** me in school or Little League practice, and I had **a knot of guilt in my throat** about what I'd done to Lenny. Still, in the cold war between my brother and me, which always **simmered just below the surface**, it felt good to **score a victory now and then**.

₅₅

(18) I read for a while in my room and fell asleep still in my baseball uniform. I **woke to** Dad banging on my door. Outside the sun had gone down, and the last, **quartz-colored** light was **draining** from the sky.

"**Yeah, no**," I said half-asleep, not sure what he'd asked.

He opened the door, came in, and turned on the light. "Where is ₆₀ your brother? **Where'd** he go?"

I sat on the edge of the bed, blinking, rubbing the **back of my hand** over my face. Mom appeared in the doorway behind him. "It's past dinner time."

³⁷ driveway:「（公道から家に通じる）私道」

³⁹ The driveway took Lenny past the outside of my room:「レニーが家の私道を歩いていくと、ぼくの部屋の外を通りかかった」

⁴¹ screen:「網戸」

⁴² Whatever, man:「なんでもいいだろう、お前」

⁴⁵ get yours:（口語）「自分でしたことの報いを受ける」

⁴⁷ must've heard: = must have heard 過去の推量。

⁴⁹ bump:「腫れ」

⁵⁰ would have plenty of chances:「多くの機会があるだろう」時制の一致で will が would になっている。

⁵¹ get back at:「～に仕返しをする」

⁵¹⁻⁵² a knot of guilt in my throat:「罪悪感で喉がつかえる感じ」

⁵³⁻⁵⁴ simmered just below the surface:「表面下でくすぶっていた」

⁵⁴ score a victory:「勝利をおさめる」

now and then:「時々」

⁵⁷ woke to:「～で目が覚めた」

⁵⁸ quartz-colored:「石英色の」

draining:「次第に色を失う」

⁵⁹ Yeah, no: 寝ぼけていて何を聞かれたのかわかっていないため、正反対の返事をしている。

⁶¹ Where'd: = Where did

⁶²⁻⁶³ back of my hand:「手の甲」

"He must've gone with Lenny," Dad said over his shoulder. "Mrs. Miller called and said she'd **swing by**. I didn't see her pull up. She must've come **though**."

Mom said, "Maybe he didn't understand when you told him he couldn't stay over."

"No, I was very clear. He doesn't listen."

The two of them went back down the hall and I heard Mom say she'd call Mrs. Miller. I **shrugged on** my nylon windbreaker and stumbled out into the living room. I heard Mom dialing on **the portable phone handset** in thc kitchen, but after a minute she told Dad there was no answer. "I'm sure it was only a misunderstanding."

Dad raised his voice: "No, he keeps doing this. We've talked about how he does this. When he gets back, he's grounded this time. No more Little League. No more nights over. No more nothing."

"Doesn't her husband have a **cell phone**? You don't know the number? Anyway, I'll call them again in a few minutes," she said, walking into their bedroom. "Calm down."

"I am calm. This is what happens when you go too **easy on** him. **Not anymore**."

I chose this moment to slip into the mudroom and quietly open the back door. I'd watched Mrs. Miller's car roll down the driveway and turn onto the road, and I knew Rob hadn't gone with them. But **telling my parents wouldn't have accomplished anything**. He would still be missing.

I was still scared of the dark and my back stiffened as I crossed the yard, but so long as I stayed on the farm there was a feeling of familiar security. I let myself into the empty pasture through the gate. Rob had collected most the baseballs, but I spotted a few more in the dusky light and picked them up, carrying them in a little pile against my chest as I walked toward the back fence, where Lenny's home run had gone into the woods. **Sure enough**, the five-gallon bucket was right where my brother must've left it before he hopped the fence. I dropped the

66 swing by:「(途中で)立ち寄る」

67 though:「けれども」Unit 1, 100行目参照。

72 shrugged on:「身をくねらせて着た」

73-74 the portable phone handset:「電話の子機」

79 cell phone:「携帯電話」1990年代アメリカでは2Gの通信サービスが提供されていた。なお、イギリスで携帯電話はmobile phoneという。

82 easy on:「〜に対して甘い」

83 Not anymore:「これ以上甘やかすのはだめだ」

87 telling my parents wouldn't have accomplished anything: = If I had told my parents that Rob hadn't gone with Lenny and Mrs. Miller, it wouldn't have accomplished anything.

95 Sure enough:(口語)「思ったとおり」

balls I'd collected into the bucket and peered into the thicket beyond the boards. A **deer track** led a few feet onto the military land before disappearing in the **ferns** and the darkness.

The last thing I wanted was to see Rob grounded, for him to be 100 dragging around the house like a beaten dog. For Dad to make him quit the Little League team, which would be the end of my playing career too. I **wanted him happy, but to treat me like his equal**, or nearly so.

⁹⁸ deer track:「鹿の足跡」

⁹⁹ ferns:「（植物の）シダ」

¹⁰⁰ The last thing I wanted ... :「もっとも望んでいないことは」この文の動詞はwas、補語はto seeとto beの並列。to beの前のfor himはto beの意味上の主語。続く1文はこの文と同じ構造になっており、The last thing I wanted was for Dad to make ... と考える。

¹⁰³ I wanted him happy, but to treat me like his equal, or nearly so:「ロブには幸せになってほしかったが、ぼくを彼と対等か、それに近い存在としてあつかってほしかった」to treatの前にwanted himを補って考える。

💬 **Expression** | 本文を参考に次の表現を英語に直す時に空所に入る語を書きなさい。

1. 彼の顔は怒りで歪んだ。

His face twisted in (　　　　　　　).

2. こっちへ来い。

Get (　　　　　　　) here.

3. そんなことをするほど馬鹿じゃない。

I knew (　　　　　　　) than to do that.

4. 馬を扱うのには母は慣れていた。

My mother was used (　　　　　　　) handling horses.

5. 少しだけ話しをしてもいいですか。

Can I have a quick（　　　　　　　）?

💡 **Comprehension** | 次の問いに答えなさい。

1. his smile froze. (ℓ.2) とありますが、どうしてこうなったのですか。

2. レニーがころんだ時の様子をまとめなさい。

3. whose lip was starting to swell. (ℓ.16) とは、どのような様子ですか。

4. I had a knot of guilt in my throat. (ℓℓ.51-52) とは、どのようなことを例えていますか。

5. Dad raised his voice: "No, he keeps doing this." (ℓ.76) のthisとは、どのようなことを指していますか。

6. "he's grounded this time." (ℓ.77) とは、どのようなことですか。

_____

7. a feeling of familiar security (ℓℓ.90-91) とは、どのようなことですか。

_____

8. The last thing I wanted was... (ℓ.100) 「ぼく」がもっとも望んでいないことは、どのようなことですか。

_____

9. which would be the end of my playing career, too. (ℓℓ.102-103) とは、どういうことか説明しなさい。

_____

10. 最後の文、I wanted him happy, but to treat me like his equal, or nearly so. (ℓ.104) には、ロブに対するどのような感情が込められていると思いますか。

_____

⇄ Discussion

1. 兄と「ぼく」の間のthe cold warが本文全体でどのように描かれているか話し合いましょう。

_____

2. なぜ父が母の名前を呼んだことが奇妙に感じられたのか、その時の家庭内の様子を話し合ってみましょう。

_____

✎ **Writing**

Write a letter of apology to a friend to whom you have done something wrong.

Grammar Guide — as if と省略

as if [though] に続く節の中にto不定詞、分詞がある場合は主語と動詞が省略されることがあります。He raised his foot as if to stomp me.(ℓ.17)は…as if (he raised) to stomp me. 「まるで彼は私を踏みつけんばかりに足を上げた」の意味になります。

Unit : 4

「ぼく（ダン）」は、夜になっても帰らない兄のロブを探しに行って砲撃演習に出くわします。そして一緒に帰宅すると家族の深刻な問題に直面します。

📖 Pre-reading

1. 演習場とはどのような場所か、調べてみましょう。

2. 日本やアメリカ、その他の国々の離婚率を調べてみましょう。

🎙 Vocabulary

次の語の定義を下記のａからｊの中から選びなさい。

| **1.** burst | **2.** instinctive | **3.** spiteful | **4.** tense | **5.** gravel |
| **6.** scurry | **7.** filthy | **8.** sob | **9.** plow | **10.** vitriol |

a. small stones, used to make a surface for paths, roads etc.

b. to cry noisily while breathing in short sudden bursts

c. not involving thought

d. to break open or apart suddenly and violently so that its contents come out

e. very cruel and angry remarks that are intended to hurt someone's feelings

f. to move quickly with short steps, especially because you are in a hurry

g. a piece of farm equipment used to turn over the earth so that seeds can be planted

h. deliberately nasty to someone in order to hurt or upset them

i. very dirty

j. to feel very anxious and worried because of something bad that might happen

(21) **I** **know now** that I wasn't **as good a brother as I could have been**. I could never tell when the **streak of** spitefulness in me would burst forth, and I **couldn't help thinking** Rob and I **would have wound up differently** if I'd been a bit tougher, **thicker-skinned. Then again,** maybe **if he'd better rewarded the trust I instinctively placed in** 5 **him?** But, as it was, I turned out to be the last child our parents would have, and so **our roles** would be the only ones we'd ever take in our staging of the eternal sibling drama, which has played out countless times in every corner of this earth, no two times the same.

And so, I climbed the fence and jumped over onto the military 10 land. When I landed in the thicket, I felt **the fear**, the certainty there was something out in the wilderness waiting for me. **Despite** the dark, I could still follow the track Rob must've taken. **The deer trail** led to a gravel road that cut through the **pitch black** forest, and following the familiar course, I came up onto the prairie. In one corner of the grassy 15 plain, I spotted **a pair of headlights**, though they were at least half a mile off. If I kept low, I wouldn't be seen.

(22) I was so tense, my heart seemed to stop as I half-jogged half-crept across the prairie, finally finding **cover** by a **patch** of trees that stood next to where the gravel road turned and led up a small hill. I 20 rested a moment, **listening for** all the awful sounds of the night, but the only thing I heard was silence. On the **crest** of the hill was a series of **trenches** Rob and I had found in the fall; ditches tall as a man, **littered with spent bullet casings** from the soldiers' **target practice**.

I **scurried** up the slope, lowered myself into the first ditch I found. 25 The rain earlier in the day had turned the bottom of the trench to mud, and I knew my shoes were already filthy while I began **duck walking** through the **branching** pathways. At the first bend, I paused and coughed into my hand.

(23) **"What do you want?"** I jumped at the voice, but **I'd known I'd** 30 **find** him out here. When I came around the corner, Rob was squatting in the dark, gently tossing **the homerun ball** in the air and catching it.

1 　I know now ... : 現在形になっていることから、この段落では「ぼく（ダン）」が現在から当時を振り返って語っていることに注意。

　as good a brother as I could have been: 名詞を修飾する形容詞（ここではgood）にas が修飾する場合、「as＋形容詞＋a＋名詞」の語順になる。ふたつ目のas以降は仮定法で「ぼくがなりえたであろう最良の弟」の意。

2 　streak of:「連続した」

3 　couldn't help thinking:「考えずにはいられなかった」　can't help ~ing = can't help but *do*　Unit 1, 78-79行目参照。

3-4 　would have wound up differently:「結果的に今とは違うふうになっていただろう」

　thicker-skinned: thick-skinned「物事に動じない」の比較級。

4-5 　Then again:「その一方」

5-6 　if he'd better rewarded the trust I instinctively placed in him?:「ぼくが本能的に彼に寄せていた信頼にもっと報いてくれていたならば？」

7 　our roles: 8行目のstaging, drama, play outとともに、人生を演劇にたとえて語っている。

11 　the fear: 恐怖の内容を同格のthe certainty [that] ... と説明している。

12 　Despite: = In spite of

13 　The deer trail: Unit 3, 98行目参照。

14 　pitch black:「漆黒の闇」pitch: タールや石油などを蒸留すると残る黒い物体。塗料などに用いる。

16 　a pair of headlights:「（基地内の）車両のヘッドライト」

19 　cover:「身を隠す場所」　　patch:「（周囲の部分とは異なる土地の）一画」

21 　listening for:「（何か聞こえないかと）耳を澄ます」

22 　crest: = top

23 　trenches:「塹壕」

23-24 　littered with:「～が散らばった」

24 　spent bullet casings:「使用済みの弾丸の薬莢（やっきょう）」　casing: 発射薬が入った真鍮や銅でできた容器。

　target practice:「射撃訓練」

25 　scurried:「小刻みに急いで歩いた」

27-28 　duck walking: アヒルのように身をかがめて外またで歩くこと。

28 　branching:「分岐している」

30 　What do you want?:「何の用だ？」

30-31 　**Q. 1**　I'd known I'd find = I (　　) known I (　　) find

32 　the homerun ball: レニーが打ったボール。Unit 2, 96行目以下参照。

"They're looking for you," I said. "They think you went home with Lenny."

"So?"   35

"So, they'll **ground** you." I **heard** voices from far off **carried up** the hill by the wind. "Listen, I'm sorry. I didn't mean for him to **bust his lip**."

(24)   He tossed the ball underhand toward me, and it landed on the ground and rolled against my shoe. "I don't care. He's fine. Maybe he   40 **deserved it** a little."

Picking up the dirty ball, its shape stretched my fingers as far as they could go. "Did you see the paratroopers?"

"**Nah**," he said, looking at the ground. "There's a couple of trucks and **a bunch of** soldiers out there. I got **pretty** close without them   45 noticing. They're just standing around, talking."

"Let's get out of here then. **I want to be able to go to practice** next week."

"Fine," Rob said, **getting to his feet**.

(25)   By then, the only light came from a **shard** of moon shining like the   50 inside of a seashell. We came down the hill where the trenches were and **hunched** beside one of the trees for a second, looking across the tall grass toward the lights at the end of the field, which glowed even brighter now. I would never have admitted **it**, but I felt safer with Rob there beside me.   55

We started across the prairie but hadn't **made it** halfway when **a bass drum thrummed in the distance**, another following a few seconds after. Both of us **seized up. A football field away**, the grass rose into the air, **the sound of the earth opening and flinging dirt and rocks in every direction**.   60

(26)   My ears rang and I yelled to Rob, "They're shooting at—"

The force of the air from the next explosion knocked me to the ground. Rob grabbed my arm, pulling me up. "**Artillery practice**. They have no idea we're out here."

³⁶ ground: Unit 3, 77行目参照。

heard ... carried up: hear（知覚動詞）＋ 目的語 ＋ 補語（過去分詞）の構文。

³⁷⁻³⁸ bust his lip:「唇を切る」Unit 3, 27行目参照。

⁴¹ deserved it:「そうなって当然だ」it = to bust his lip

⁴² Picking up the dirty ball: = I picked up the dirty ball　独立分詞構文で主節の主語と異なる場合は表記するのが通例だが、ここでは "I" が省略されている。

⁴⁴ Nah:（口語）No

⁴⁵ a bunch of:「一団の」

pretty:（口語）「かなり」（副詞）

⁴⁷ I want to be able to go to practice: 父が怒って言っていたように、ロブが野球禁止になってしまうと、ぼくも野球ができなくなってしまうことを心配している。Unit 3, 77-78行目参照。

⁴⁹ getting to his feet:「立ち上がる」

⁵⁰ shard:「かけら」shard 以下、読み上げるとsの音が繰り返される頭韻（alliteration）の技法が用いられている。

⁵² hunched:「背中を丸めた」

⁵⁴ it: この後の but 以下の内容を指す。

⁵⁶ made it:（口語）「（目的地に）到達した」

⁵⁶⁻⁵⁷ a bass drum thrummed in the distance: 最初の砲弾の発射音。1発目はフットボールフィールド一面ぐらい離れた距離に（58-60行目）、続く2発目はふたりのそばに落ちる（62-63行目）。

⁵⁸ seized up:「動きを止めた」

A football field away:「フットボールフィールド一面ぐらい遠くに」　football:「アメリカンフットボール」

⁵⁹⁻⁶⁰ the sound of the earth opening and flinging dirt and rocks in every direction:「地面が割れて、あらゆる方向に土と岩を弾き飛ばす音」

⁶³ Artillery practice:「砲撃演習」

Unit: 4

Two more bass drums sounded. Rob ran, dragging me behind 65
him. The shockwave of the next blast hit from the other side, and my
face was suddenly wet. I thought dirt rained down on us, but when I
touched my cheek, it was too dark to see if my fingers were streaked
with mud. I wanted to lie down on the gravel and sob, but Rob had my
wrist in a **vice grip**. He pulled me across the prairie like a **plow**. 70

When we finally reached the other side, I panted, "Oh, god. Oh,
god."

"They never got within fifty **yards**. Those weren't **frag rounds**
anyway."

I didn't believe him. I wiped my face with my palms, **blew the** 75
snot from my nose.

(27)   As we walked back to the farm, I realized I was still holding the
baseball he'd given me. I tried to imitate my brother and act like I
hadn't been terrified out on the prairie, but I **couldn't help looking**
back over my shoulder again and again. I tried to think of what to tell 80
our parents instead, how to hide my muddy shoes.

We followed a trail that led back onto the farm and came up behind
the house, where the light from the mudroom windows **fell** across the
backyard. Rob stopped by the side of Dad's van and squatted down in
the shadows. 85

I said, "Okay, you were getting all the balls like you'd been told
and didn't realize how late it was. Let me explain it."

He put a hand on my shoulder, and even though it was dark I could
tell when he **nodded toward** the house and the window that looked into
the mudroom. "They don't even remember we're gone." 90

(28)   I looked more carefully and saw the back of Dad's head inside.
The door to the kitchen stood open and Mom was there. She was red in
the face from shouting, and her hair was **mussed**. Dad was pointing at
the ground and then at her, yelling something back. The whole house
echoed with their fight, though I couldn't **make out** what they said. **I** 95
could tell, mixed into their vitriol, were plenty of the words they'd

70 vice grip:「万力のように強くつかんで」

plow:「鋤」この文ではpの音の頭韻が見られる。

73 yards: 1ヤード＝ 約91.4センチ。

frag rounds:「全方向に飛びちる榴弾」fragはfragmentation grenadeの略。

75 I didn't believe him:「彼の言ったことを信じなかった」

75-76 blew the snot from my nose:「鼻をかんだ」

79 couldn't help looking: 3行目の注を参照。

83 fell:「（光が）〜に射した」主語はthe light。

89 nodded toward:「〜の方に向かってあごをしゃくった」

93 mussed:「（髪が）くしゃくしゃになった」

95 make out: = understand

95-96 I could tell ... : = I could tell that ... 直前の I couldn't make out ... と対比されている。

96-97 mixed into their vitriol, were plenty of the words they'd forbidden us from saying: = plenty of the words they'd forbidden us from saying were mixed into their vitriol.倒置構文になっておりwereの主語はplenty以下。(Unit 1, 82行目以下では、父がロブに対して汚い言葉を使わないように言っている。)

mixed into their vitriol:「辛辣な言葉に混ざって」両親のかわす辛辣な言葉のやりとりを表すのにvitriol（元々は火薬の原料にも使われる「硝酸」の意味）という単語が使われており、戦場のイメージと重なる。ふたりは軍事演習の榴弾から必死に逃れてきたが、家庭ももはや平穏な場所ではなかった。

Unit: 4

forbidden us from saying. Plenty of gosh-darns and forget yous, but the real thing. It was like watching two strangers, two people you are glad you will never have to meet. But, of course, we had to go back in there. 100

(29)　　After a minute, Mom reached out, grabbed the handle of the door to the kitchen, and **yanked** it shut **so hard** the glass of the mudroom window shook. Then **Dad turned and walked out of the window frame,** and the door to the garage slammed shut. **It was then that** I realized Rob had understood something about our parents, about our 105 family, something dark and unhappy that I'd been completely **blind to.** It was there though, **emanating out of** the house like the light from the mudroom. This was his way of showing me, but as we crouched in the dark, **I wished he never had.**

97-98　Plenty of gosh-darns and forget yous, but the real thing: 文になっておらず名詞句のみである。gosh-darn は goddamn「ちくしょう」の婉曲的な表現。forget you は「勝手にしろ」という罵りの言葉。複数形になっており、繰り返し使われていることがわかる。gosh-darns and forget yous は前文の plenty of the words they'd forbidden us from saying の具体的な内容だが、but the real thing とあることから、gosh-darn や forget you より強い直接的な表現が使われていたことが示唆されている。

102　yanked:「ぐいと引っ張った」

　　　so hard: = so hard that

103-104　**Q. 2** ⟫　Dad turned and walked out of the window frame とはどういうことですか。

104　It was then that ... :「〜したのはまさにその時だった」強調構文。

106　blind to:「〜に気づいていない」

107　emanating out of:「(光などが) 〜から発せられる」

109　I wished he never had: = I wished he never had shown me something about their parents ... 104-106 行目を参照。

💬 **Expression**   本文を参考に次の表現を英語に直す時に空所に入る語を書きなさい。

1. 彼の冗談に笑わざるを得なかった。

    I couldn't (   ) laughing at his joke.

2. 私は彼が間違っているとわかった。

    It turned (   ) that he made a terrible mistake.

3. あたりが暗すぎて、私は指が怪我しているかわからなかった。

    It was (   ) dark to see if my fingers were injured.

4. それを説明させてください。

    (   ) me explain it.

5. 私達両方とも固まってしまった。

    (   ) of us seized up.

💡 **Comprehension**   次の問いに答えなさい。

1. so our roles would be the only ones we'd ever take in our staging of the eternal sibling drama (ℓℓ.7-8) とは、具体的にどのようなことを意味していますか。

    _____

2. no two times the same. (ℓ.9) とは、どのような意味ですか。

    _____

3. I felt the fear, (ℓ.11) の恐怖の内容はどのようなものだったか、説明しなさい。

    _____

4. 丘の頂上にあった塹壕はどのようなものでしたか、説明しなさい。

    _____

5. Maybe he deserved it a little. (ℓℓ.40-41) はどうしてだと思いますか。

    _____

6. By then, the only light came from a shard of moon shining like the inside of a seashell. (ℓℓ.50-51) とは、どのような光景を表した表現ですか。

_____

7. I couldn't help looking back over my shoulder again and again. (ℓℓ.79-80) には、ぼくのどのような気持ちがあらわれていますか。

_____

8. They don't even remember we're gone. (ℓ.90) とは、They が指すものを明らかにしてどのような様子だったのかを説明しなさい。

_____

9. Plenty of gosh-darns and forget yours, but the real thing. (ℓℓ.97-98) には、どのような情景が示されていますか。

_____

10. It was then that I realized Rob had understood something about our parents, (ℓℓ.104-105) からわかることはなんですか。

_____

⇄ Discussion

1. 両親のひどい言い争いの様子を見た時の「ぼく」の気持ちを話し合いましょう。

_____

2. 「ぼく」のロブに対する思いが表現されている箇所を抜きだして、その気持ちを話し合ってみましょう。

_____

✎ Writing

Write about your experience and feelings about being in the dark.

Grammar Guide —— 仮定法過去完了　過去の事実に対する仮定

Rob and I would have wound up differently if I'd been a bit tougher, thicker-skinned.(ℓℓ.3-4)「ぼくがもう少し物に動じない性格であったら、ロブとぼくは最後にはもっと違ったふうになっていたであろうに。」には自分はその当時タフでもなかったし、すぐに動揺してしまう弱さがあったので、その過去の事実の反対の仮定をするために条件節に過去完了を用いて仮定法過去完了で表現しています。

Chapter 2

One Flew East, One Flew West

(30) If the first story in this text was one of late childhood, then this piece is about adolescence, those years when a young person's world begins to open with possibilities that they are often not yet equipped to handle. Not the least of these possibilities is the bewildering fact of romantic attraction—those furtive glances at the boy or girl who draws your eye, the catch in your throat, the thin layer of sweat on the back of your neck.

In this case, the setting is a day in a typical small-town school. This piece and the one that follows, show something of the diversity of American life: the blending of people from different cultures and ethnicities, classes and experiences. The possibility of community across these boundaries is, to my mind, the true beauty of the country.

This piece uses a more complex narrative, weaving together several voices that vary in tone and expression. In this way, the structure resembles the dramatic performance, which is at the heart of the story and from which it takes its title.

Chapter 1が、もうそろそろ幼い子どもではいられなくなる年代を扱っているとすれば、Chapter 2は思春期の物語です。この年ごろは、若い人の世界がさまざまな可能性に開かれようとする時期ですが、その可能性を伸ばしていく準備ができているかというと、そうでもないことが多いのです。この「可能性」のなかでも相当重要なのが、恋愛感情で惹かれるという、どうしていいか分からなくなるような事実です。つまり思わず目で追ってしまう男の子や女の子に向けるまなざし、言葉が出てこない喉のつかえ、うなじにうっすらかいた汗などのことです。

この物語は、田舎町の典型的な学校のある一日を描いたものです。この話とあとに続くChapter 3は、アメリカの生活における多様性の片鱗を示しています。異なる文化、民族、階級、経験の人々の混淆、そして、そういう壁を越えてコミュニティを形成する可能性、これこそが、アメリカという国の真の美しさだと私には思えるのです。

この物語の語りかたはChapter 1よりも複雑で、調子や表情の異なる複数の「声」が織り合わさっています。この点で、この話の構造は、物語の中心となっている劇の上演に似ています。そして、物語のタイトルも、その劇にちなんだものです。

Unit : 5

このUnitでは、中高時代のロブと「ぼく（ダン）」の生活が描かれます。教師であるコセンティーノ先生が後になって語っている部分の表現に気をつけましょう。

📖 Pre-reading

1. 禁煙に向けた社会の動きについて、アメリカと日本、および他の国の状況を調べてみましょう。

2. アメリカ合衆国全体とワシントン州のethnicity（民族的背景）について調べてみましょう。

🎙 Vocabulary

次の語の定義を下記のａからｊの中から選びなさい。

1. sneak	**2.** criminal	**3.** ban	**4.** janitor	**5.** burden
6. congregation	**7.** weave	**8.** reel back	**9.** suspension	**10.** shove

a. a group of people gathered together in a church

b. someone who is involved in illegal activities

c. to step backwards suddenly and almost fall over, especially after being hit or getting a shock

d. something difficult or worrying that you are responsible for

e. to push someone or something in a rough or careless way, using your hands or shoulders

f. to say that something must not be done, seen, used etc.

g. when someone is not allowed to go to school, do their job, or take part in an activity for a period of time as a punishment

h. (informal) to secretly take something small or unimportant

i. someone whose job is to look after a school or other large building

j. to move somewhere by turning and changing direction a lot

(31) Julie **Cosentino** snuck cigarettes in her car. There wasn't anything **saying** teachers weren't allowed to smoke, and this was before **the State** began treating smokers like low-level criminals, banning cigarettes from all public buildings, increasing tobacco taxes, raising smokers' **insurance premiums**. Back then there was even an 5 ashtray for the two **janitors** who smoked outside the **woodshop**, where the students couldn't see unless they walked around the side of the building. But none of the other teachers at Rainier **Middle and High School** smoked, and it was just one more thing marking her out as different. **Along with her clothes**, and her hair, and the books she 10 taught in her classes. So, she went to the **faculty lot** out back when she needed a break. She certainly didn't want to give the rest of the staff more reason to **judge her**. In addition to commuting in from "**the city**," which she thought of as her cute little town, she also carried the burden of replacing Fred Suden, **beloved** English and French teacher, who'd 15 suffered an **aneurysm** two months ago. It was good he was **out of the coma** and was expected to regain full function, **but still**.

(32) Before this, **she'd been substitute teaching** near **Tacoma**, in **schools with metal detectors and armed guards** and class sizes larger than most **church congregations**, though this probably wasn't true in 20 Rainier, **where churches outnumbered gas stations**, outnumbered restaurants and grocery stores. **Regardless**, she was happy to have a reason to be out of **Olympia**, where her recently unemployed ex-husband lived and **had far too much time on his hands to park** in front of her house and call her over and over until she had to unplug the 25 **landline** and turn off her cell phone.

(33) She wanted to move back to **Seattle**, where she was from, but there were too many teachers in the State and permanent positions were hard to find. Luckily, Rainier had given her a full-year contract, as Fred's recovery would take at least that long. **Given** his health, there'd 30 been **talk he might retire**; if she did a good job, Principal Brown could keep her on full time. **The middle school her son, Darren, attended**

1 Cosentino: イタリア系の名前。レイニアのような小さな田舎町におけるコセンティーノ先生の社会的な立ち位置を考えるうえで参考にしたい。

2 **Q. 1** ▶▶ saying は言い換えると次のどちらでしょう。

          A. that says   B. as it says

3 the State: 物語の舞台となっているワシントン州。

5 insurance premiums: 「保険料」

6 janitors: 「管理人、用務員」

   woodshop: 「管理人室、作業場」

8-9 Middle and High School: middle school は小学校6年から中学校2年に、high schoolは中学校3年から高等学校3年までの4年間に相当する。名称からして、この学校は中高一貫校である。

10 Along with her clothes ... : これは完全な文になっていないことに注意。

11 faculty lot: 「教員用の駐車場」

13 judge her: 「彼女がどういう人物であるか判断を下す（主に批判的に）」

   the city: あとに出てくるOlympiaを指す。この地域で the（何を指すかについての理解が話し手と聞き手のあいだで共有されていることを示す）がつく city と言えばオリンピアに決まるので、定冠詞がついている。

15 beloved: 「みなに愛されている」

16 aneurysm: 「動脈瘤」

16-17 out of the coma: 「昏睡状態から醒めて」

17 but still: 「それでもなお」あとにhe could not moveやhe was in bedなどが省略されていると考える。

18 she'd been substitute teaching = she had been a substitute teacher

   substitute teacher: 「代替講師、臨時的任用教員」

   Tacoma: ワシントン州の港湾都市。

19 schools with metal detectors and armed guards: 「金属探知機や武器をもった警備員がいる」

20 church congregations: 「教会の礼拝に集まる人々」

21 where churches outnumbered gas stations, ... : 「教会のほうがガソリンスタンドよりも多い」

22 Regardless: 「とにかく」

23 Olympia: ワシントン州の州都。

24 had far too much time on his hands to park: コセンティーノ先生の元・夫が暇すぎる様子を強調して表現している。to park が time を説明していると考えると自然な流れで読める。

26 landline: 「固定電話」

27 Seattle: 「シアトル」（ワシントン州の大都市）

30 Given: 「〜のことを考慮すると」

31 talk he might retire: 「フレッドが引退（辞職）するのではないか、といううわさ」 talk のあとにthatを補って考える。

32 The middle school her son, Darren, attended: school のあとに which を補うと考えやすい。また、Darrenは her son を説明するために挿入されている。

Unit: 5

was on the way, and she liked her students and the drama club, which she'd taken over.

(34)   I learned these details years later, when I **ran into Ms. C** in **the** 35 **Safeway**, bought her a coffee at the little cafe inside the supermarket, and asked her to tell me everything she remembered of those days. But on that Monday, she was in her car when she saw Lenny come around the corner of the school followed by **another boy**. **The other boy** talked and **pointed**, **jabbing** Lenny's chest with his finger, and Lenny shoved 40 him, **sending him reeling** back.

The other boy **rushed forward**, **hands fisted** at his sides, and she was out of her car, **flinging her cigarette to the gravel** and crossing the lot, shouting, "Hey now. Hey now, **there**."

They hesitated for a second, enough time for her to get between 45 them. She put her hand on the shoulder of the boy who was about to **throw a punch**. "**What's a matter with you?**"

"He started it," Lenny said.

"**You did shove him**." To the other boy she didn't know, she said, "Name. Tell me your name." 50

The other boy **looked away**, and she demanded his name again. He said, "I'm Rob Overton."

"Overton?" **She shook her head**. Everyone was **related** in this town, **a tangle of connections** that caught you **like a spider's web**. "You know, if you hit him, it's a month's **suspension**." 55

"**What do I care**? Football season's over."

(35) Lenny came into the **common room**, looking over his shoulder to see if Rob was behind him. He must've still been **getting a talking to** from Ms. C **though** because he wasn't there. Lenny **wove** through 60 the tables in the common room, where kids were sitting and talking, others were **putting down** quick breakfasts of yogurt or **microwaved Hot Pockets**, and **a couple** had out textbooks and were trying to finish their homework before **first period**.

35 ran into:「偶然出くわす」

Ms. C: コセンティーノ先生のこと。中高生が教師にあだ名をつけるように頭文字で呼ぶことがあるところから、この物語では生徒目線でこのように表記されている。

35-36 the Safeway: アメリカの大手スーパーマーケットチェーン。

39 **Q. 2 ▶** another と the other はどちらも「もう一人の」の意味ですが、違いは何でしょう。

40 pointed:「指を突きつけた」 jabbing:「すばやく突いて」

41 sending him reeling:「後ろによろめかせた」

42 rushed forward:「激しく詰め寄った」

hands fisted:「両手を拳に固めて」(fist は「(手を)拳にする」の意の他動詞。過去分詞で受動的に hands を修飾している)

43 flinging her cigarette to the gravel:「タバコを砂利道に投げ捨てながら」

44 there:「ちょっと、君たち」

47 throw a punch:「パンチを出す、ぶん殴る」

What's a matter with you?: 標準英語であれば、the matter だが、口語的にやや崩れた表現。

49 You did shove him.: did shove は shoved よりも強い表現。「君が押したのも確かだよね」くらいの意。

51 looked away:「顔をそむけた」反抗的な態度を示している。

53 She shook her head:「(信じられないというように)首を振った」

Q. 3 ▶ related は次のどちらの意味でしょう。
A.「親戚・家族である」 B.「何か関係がある」

54 a tangle of connections:「複雑にもつれた関係性」。関係節を伴う名詞句が、文のほかの部分から独立して置かれ、前の文の内容を言い換えている。

like a spider's web:「蜘蛛の網のように」語り手がこの町の人間関係をどう捉えているか、比喩的に表されている。

55 suspension:「停学」

56 What do I care? = I do not care at all. この少年は野球とフットボールの選手なので、シーズン中に停学をくらうと試合に出られない、などの目にあうが、今はシーズンではないため、そんなことは気にしない、と言っている。

58 common room:「休憩室、談話室」

59-60 getting a talking to:「説教をくらって」

60 though:「でも」 その前の「ロブが来ていないか確かめた」ことと「コセンティーノ先生から説教をくらっているに違いない」ことが逆接で結ばれている。

wove: weave の過去形。「～の間を縫うように進む」

62 putting down:「(口に)詰め込む」

microwaved:「電子レンジで温めた、レンチンした」(microwave は他動詞で、「電子レンジで調理する、温める」)

63 Hot Pockets: 具材を包んだ簡単なパイの商標。ここにあるように、レンジで温めて食べる。

a couple:「ふたり組」(必ずしも日本語の「カップル」だとは限らない)

64 first period:「1時間目」

Unit : 5

He walked over to the drama set, where I'd opened the curtains a ⁶⁵ few feet and was checking the **painted backdrop** as I went through the long list of tasks I still needed to finish. He was playing a mental patient named Harding in the play, which was opening that night. Looking up at me from **the lip of the stage**, he said, "**Dude**, what's wrong with your brother?" ⁷⁰

(36) Since **the divorce**, Rob had started wearing his black hair **with a stark part down the middle**, **his acne had worsened**, and he'd stopped smiling. Even though Mom had forbidden it, he bought rap CDs with the *EXPLICIT* **sticker** on the front and only **bothered** to keep up his grades in history and social studies, **where Mr. Wilson and Mr. Lycker,** ⁷⁵ **the baseball and football coaches, were the teachers**. I crouched down toward Lenny, and asked, "What happened?"

"He said I was **flirting with** Shanae. Yeah right. Nick had a straw and was blowing on the back of her neck in **bio**, but she saw me when she turned around. It was her mistake." ⁸⁰

(37) Rob and Shanae had been **going out** for maybe a year. In the spring one of his freshmen classmates had **called her a name**, and Rob grabbed the kid by the throat and held him against the wall. He'd managed to **get off with** an **in-school suspension**, but with baseball season over and football still **a summer away**, he hadn't seemed too ⁸⁵ **bothered**. Mom considered taking him to a therapist, but he refused to go. Sometimes I wanted to act like I didn't know him.

"I'll let him know," I said. "Just stay away from him. That's what I do."

"**Whatever, man**. Tell him to **chill out**." ⁹⁰

He walked away and disappeared around a corner. In my mind, I followed him down the hallway, to his locker. He walked past Ms. C's classroom, which connected to the backstage area, and past the door to Mrs. Lapman's classroom, where Randa was *estudiando Español*.

(38) Randa was new to Rainier Middle and High School. Her parents ⁹⁵ were both engineers, originally from Syria, though **I only knew this**

66 painted backdrop: 芝居の背景を描いた幕。

69 the lip of the stage: ステージの真下で、客席の床と接している部分。

Dude: 「なあ、おい」などの呼びかけ。

71 the divorce: 第1話で語られていたロブと「ぼく（ダン）」の両親が離婚していることが語られている。

71-72 with a stark part down the middle: 「髪を真ん中できっちりと分けて」

72 his acne had worsened: acneは「にきび」ストレスが肌に表れていることを示している。

74 *EXPLICIT* sticker: 内容が性的・暴力的であるため、保護者に対して注意を促すためにCDに貼られたシール。実際には、ここにあるように逆効果となっていた。

bothered: 「（面倒なことを）何とか〜した」

75-76 where Mr. Wilson and Mr. Lycker, the baseball and football coaches, were the teachers: 野球とフットボールの顧問の先生の授業だけは何とか成績を落とさないようにしていることから、ロブの学校生活が運動を中心に回っていることを表している（*Cf.* 56行目の註）。

78 flirting with: 「ちょっかいを出す」

79 bio: 「生物の時間」

81 going out: 「つきあう」

82 called her a name: 「ののしる、悪口を言う」

84 get off with: 「〜で済む」

in-school suspension: 「学内での謹慎」

85 a summer away: 「夏が終わるまでない」（フットボールのシーズンは秋から冬にかけて）

86 bothered: ここでは、「気にする」

90 Whatever: 「どうでもいいけど、とにかく」（投げやりな間投詞）

man: 比較的カジュアルな呼びかけ。

chill out: 「頭を冷やす」

94 *estudiando Español*: = studying Spanish（スペイン語）

96-97 I only knew this because she'd told me: 「ランダが教えてくれなければ分からなかった」

because she'd told me and I couldn't have found Syria on a map even if the prize for doing so had been **the slowest, movie-style kiss** with her, an experience I very badly wanted, **even if I didn't dare say so**.

This desire, and **the fear and excitement at what might follow**, filled me like a balloon, **until a single word, a stray breath might pop me**. So far, **all Randa and I had done** was **hold hands**, and briefly, for a splinter of a second, touch lips. It hadn't been a kiss when, on Friday after school, she'd given me a peck—that was the right word for it, **a *peck***, not a proper kiss—right before my brother **pulled up** behind me in his car with the window rolled down and honked the horn saying, "Break it up, **love birds**." I jumped at the horn and **went a tomato color** as I turned to get in the passenger seat.

98 the slowest, movie-style kiss:「映画みたいな、すごく情熱的なキス」 この slowest の最上級は何かとの比較ではなく、「とても…」の意。

99 even if I didn't dare say so:「とても口に出しては言えなかったにせよ」

100 the fear and excitement at what might follow:「キスの後に続くものに対して感じる興奮と、怖いような気持ち」。「ぼく（語り手）」は中2くらいの設定なので、自分が未経験の恋愛の身体的な側面については興奮ばかりでなく、おずおずとした気持ちも持っている。

101-102 until a single word, a stray breath might pop me:「何か一言でもしゃべるか、ほんのふっと息を吹きこむかするだけで、はじけてしまいそうな」

102 all Randa and I had done:「ランダとぼくがしたのは〜だけだった」

hold hands: 本来なら to hold hands だが、口語ではこの to はしばしば省略される。

104-105 a peck :「ついばむようなキス」 イタリックにすることで、そのあとの proper kiss と対比して、これがほんの軽い接触であったことを強調している。

105 pulled up:「（車を）停める」

107 love birds: 人前でもいちゃつくカップルのこと。ここでは「おふたりさん」といった呼びかけ。

Q.4 went a tomato color の went の意味は次のどちらでしょう。
A.「（色、状態などが）変わる」
B.「出かける」

💬 Expression

本文を参考に次の表現を英語に直す時に空所に入る語を書きなさい。

1. 少年はまさに殴りかかろうとしていた。

The boy was (　　　　　　　) to throw a punch.

2. どうしたの。

What's the (　　　　　　　) with you?

3. どうでもいいことだ。

What do I (　　　　　　　)?

4. どうしたの。（どこか悪いの？）

What's (　　　　　　　) with you?

5. 級友が彼女の悪口を言っていた。

Her classmates called her a (　　　　　　　).

💡 Comprehension

次の問いに答えなさい。

1. She certainly didn't want to give the rest of the staff more reason to judge her. (ℓℓ.12-13) とありますが、彼女のことを判断する材料にはどのようなものがありましたか。

2. Fred Suden とは、どのような人ですか。

3. in schools with metal detectors and armed guards (ℓℓ.18-19) からどのような学校だと考えられますか。

4. コセンティーノ先生の前の夫はあまりにも暇で、どんなことをしましたか。

5. コセンティーノ先生がレイニア校に勤務していて良かった点は何でしたか。

6. Football season's over. (ℓ.56) とありますが、なぜこのようなことを言ったのですか。

7. only bothered to keep up his grades in history and social studies, (ℓℓ.74-75) とありますが、なぜ歴史と社会の成績だけ維持しようと頑張ったのですか。

8. Mom considered taking him to a therapist. (ℓ.86) とありますがどうしてセラピストのところに連れて行こうとしたのですか。

9. even if I didn't dare say so. (ℓ.99) とは、「ぼく（ダン）」が口に出して言えないと思ったことは何ですか。

10. I jumped at the horn and went a tomato color (ℓ.107) とは、具体的にどのような状態のことですか。

Unit: 5

⇄ **Discussion**

1. コセンティーノ先生は、オリンピアでどのような暮らしをしていましたか、話し合ってみましょう。

2. ロブは、両親の離婚後どのように変わってしまったか、それを示す本文の箇所を指摘しながら話し合いましょう。

✎ Writing

Choose a teacher you met in your school days. Describe that person in detail.

Grammar Guide ── 関係副詞の非制限用法

コンマの後の where は前にある場所について挿入的、追加的に情報を加える非制限的用法です。and there で置き換えるとわかりやすくなります。

One Flew East, One Flew West «2»

Unit: 6

「ぼく（ダン）」のガールフレンドであるランダは、コセンティーノ先生が顧問を務める演劇部に入っています。そこでの活動、「ぼく」との関係、他の友人の様子を中心に「ぼく」の中学校時代が描かれています。

📖 Pre-reading

1. アメリカの高校や大学で外国語がどのように学ばれているのか、調べてみましょう

2. ジャック・ニコルソンという俳優について、調べてみましょう。

🎙 Vocabulary

次の語の定義を下記のａからｊの中から選びなさい。

1. yell	2. hassle	3. curb	4. sense(n.)	5. bewilder
6. varsity	7. sigh	8. swoon	9. heave	10. tolerate

a. (American English) the main team that represents a university, college, or school in a sport

b. feeling that it exists or is true, without being told or having proof

c. to confuse someone

d. to pull or lift something very heavy with one great effort

e. to shout or say something very loudly, especially because you are frightened, angry, or excited

f. to fall to the ground because you have been affected by an emotion or shock

g. to allow people to do, say, or believe something without criticizing or punishing them

h. (spoken) something that is annoying, because it causes problems or is difficult to do

i. (American English) the raised edge of a road, between where people can walk and cars can drive

j. to breathe in and out making a long sound, especially because you are bored, disappointed, tired etc.

(39) Randa was **running lines** instead of practicing for her Spanish quiz because she'd already taken three semesters of the language at Evergreen Middle School and was top of her class in this town, **which her parents had said would be much, much better for her**. More space, they said, a real yard, closer to nature, smaller classes. What they hadn't said was fifteen-minutes to **the closest thing to a real town**; they hadn't mentioned boys who smelled like wet dogs, and an "**advanced**" band that couldn't get through *Boléro* without the music director stopping them three times to yell at the percussionists.

Thank God for Ms. C, though not for Mr. Suden's accident. She was sorry for him. She'd told me how, a few days after she started here, she saw him **go stiff and fall down the stairs**, and someone had dropped a milk carton and it mixed with the blood. But the one good thing to come out of it all had been Ms. C, who came from someplace where they had a real drama program, not just annual performances of *A Christmas Carol*.

(40) Ms. C had decided on *One Flew Over the Cuckoo's Nest* for the winter play, and **she'd cast against gender** for several of the roles and cut out all **the racial stuff**, saying it **dated** the whole thing. Chief Bromden became Mr. Bromden and Nurse Ratched became Dr. Ratched, played by Philip, one of the few friends Randa had made and the only gay boy in the whole school.

Randa had **landed** the role of Randall P. McMurphy and was **the only middle schooler** in the main cast. She'd spent the last month and a half watching the Jack Nicholson movie **on loop**, trying to **capture his lean physicality**. She had a length of gauze she used to flatten her chest, a big rubber band to pull her hair back, and **a black beanie** she rolled down to her ears.

(41) The first-period bell rang, and lockers slammed, doors closed, and kids **ran down** the halls. I'd gotten permission to skip my first three classes and I walked by Randa's classroom on my way to the woodshop to return the brushes I'd used to paint the backdrop, listening to Mrs.

1 running lines:「台本のセリフの読み合わせをする」

4-5 which her parents had said would be much, much better for her: her parents had said が挿入されている。

6-7 the closest thing to a real town:「本当の街にせいぜい近いと言えるような町」

8 "advanced": 引用符がついていることで、「上級」と言っても名ばかりの、という皮肉が込められている。

Boléro: モーリス・ラヴェル Maurice Ravel (1875-1937) 作曲のバレエ音楽（初演1928年）。パーカッションは曲を通じて同じリズムを刻むので、それがうまくいかないというのは、相当レベルが低いことを示している。前註も参照のこと。

10 Thank God for Ms. C:「コセンティーノ先生がいてくれてよかった」

12 go stiff and fall down the stairs:「身体を硬直させて、階段を転がり落ちた」

16 *A Christmas Carol*: チャールズ・ディケンズ Charles Dickens (1812-70) 作の小説 (1843)。クリスマスの日に守銭奴の主人公が精霊の訪れにより改心する物語。ここでは、ありきたりで無難な演題として挙げられている。

17 *One Flew Over the Cuckoo's Nest*: ケン・キージー Ken Kesey (1935-2001) 作の小説 (1962)。1975年にジャック・ニコルソン主演で映画化され、アカデミー賞を受賞した。

18 she'd cast against gender:「元々の配役とは異なる性別でキャスティングをしていた」she'd = she had cast は原形と過去分詞形が同じ。

19 the racial stuff:「人種にかかわる内容」

dated :「古くさく感じさせてしまう」

23 landed :「（役などを）獲得する、得る」

23-24 the only middle schooler:「中等部から選ばれたキャストはランダだけだった」middle school と high school が同じ学校（中高一貫校をイメージするとよい）で、ほかのキャストは全員 high school から選ばれていた、ということ。

25 on loop:「何度も繰り返して」

25-26 capture his lean physicality:「しなやかな身のこなしを自分のものにする」

27 a black beanie:「黒くてつばのないニット帽」

30 ran down:「走って向こうへ行く」 この down は上下ではなく、話者から遠ざかることを示している。

Lapman saying, *Sientense*, *sientense*…

(42)   When she turned up at Rainier, Randa had told me she had a boyfriend back in Olympia. Leon was in high school, he was "completely cool," and they'd kissed and well, other stuff, she'd said, **trailing off**. I wanted to know what other stuff, but I also **didn't**, so instead I got her to tell me why she hated the town, **which she clearly did**. Her reasons were the same things I hated about it, and then I asked what bands she liked, which were **The Hive Singers** and **Bikini Kill** and a bunch of Olympia bands **I didn't know that she listed** as I imagined her in the arms of some **Matt Dillon lookalike** who drove a restored **Dodge Charger** and wore a leather jacket. I'd had my first girlfriend the year before, but we'd only kissed, **a few chaste meetings of the mouths**. We'd **fallen out of touch** over the summer and **when eighth grade started** in September, we both pretended **it** hadn't happened and avoided eye contact.

"**You're not seeing anyone, are you**?" Randa asked, one day after rehearsal.

I'd been lying on the stage, **legs dangling over the edge**, but I sat up, looking around to confirm she was indeed talking to me. "**Nah**," I said.

"Lucky you. Sometimes **it's** more hassle than it's worth."

"I know what you mean," I said, rubbing the back of my neck. I had no idea what she meant.

(43)   But she'd stopped mentioning Leon over the past few weeks. Then on Saturday, **she had a bad dress rehearsal**, and I stuck around while everyone else was changing backstage and gently reminded her not to get flustered if she forgot a line, the audience wouldn't notice. Her eyes shined like marbles, and I told her not to let her confidence break and also repeated a few other things I'd heard Ms. C say to the actors. Later, Randa walked out with me even though my brother wasn't there yet to pick me up in Mom's old Mazda, **which it seemed he was going to inherit** now that he had his student driver's license. When we got to

33 *Sientense*: スペイン語で「席について」の意。

36 trailing off:「最後まではっきり言わなかった」

37 didn't:

> **Q.1** このあとに省略されているのは、次のどちらでしょう。
>
> A. want
>
> B. know

38 which she clearly did: (= she hated the town)「ランダがこの町を嫌っていたのは明らかだった」which の先行詞は前の内容。

40 The Hive Singers: The Hives というスウェーデンのロック・グループ。

Bikini Kill: 1990年にオリンピアで結成されたパンク・ロックのガールズバンド。

41 I didn't know that she listed: I didn't know も that she listed もどちらも Olympia bands を修飾している。

42 Matt Dillon lookalike :「マット・ディロンそっくりのヤツ」 マット・ディロン (1964 -) はアメリカの俳優。幅広い役をこなすが、ここにあるように、短髪でやや強面の印象が強い。

42-43 Dodge Charger: 当時はクライスラー社の一部門だった「ドッジ」というブランドの車種。ハイパフォーマンスな乗用車。1970年前後のものが有名なので、ここでも restored (レストアされた) と書かれている。趣味で古い車をいじってレストアするような男性であることが示されている。

44 a few chaste meetings of the mouths:「唇が軽く触れるだけの、なんてことないキスを2,3回しただけ」

45 fallen out of touch:「何となく会わないようになってしまった」

when eighth grade started: アメリカの学校は新しい学年が9月に始まる。

46 **Q.2** it が指すものは何でしょうか。

48 You're not seeing anyone, are you?:「今、だれともつきあってない (＝彼女いない) よね?」

50 legs dangling over the edge:「舞台の縁から足をブラブラさせて」

51 Nah: No が口語的に崩れた形。

53 it's: it は誰かとつきあっていること、彼氏／彼女がいること。

57 she had a bad dress rehearsal,:「本番通りの衣装で行うリハーサルでうまくいかなかった」

63-64 which it seemed he was going to inherit: It seemed をいったん (　　) に入れて考えてみるとよい。

Unit: 6

the curb, she took my hand and **pecked me on the lips**.   65

(44) On Monday morning, I floated down the hall thinking about this moment, when I heard Mr. Lycker shout, "I said stop right there, **mister**."

I'd sensed him moving past me, coffee cup in hand, blue jeans   70
over **steel-toed boots**, but I hadn't realized he was talking to me.

"I saw you come out of my **shop**, son. What're you doing in there? Why are you not in class?"

"Returning those old paintbrushes," I said, bewildered. "Getting ready for tonight."   75

"You're not in the play." Ms. C had recruited his son, Steven, **a varsity linebacker**, for the role of Bromden because he could lift the broken air-conditioning unit that I'd painted and fixed up to look like an electrical panel. I got the sense **Mr. Lycker was none too happy about his son being in a play**.   80

"I made the set," I said. "I'm stage manager."

(45) From my grades and my interests, the school counselor had suggested I follow the "**college track**" starting next year, and this meant I would never take health class or **non-AP math** or history or **woodshop** with Mr. Lycker, though he still occasionally **liked to stop**   85
me in the hall and give me his emptiest stare through his thick-rimmed glasses, like he was doing now, just to prove he had some sort of **power** over me.

"Very well, son. Carry on," he said finally, and went into the shop.

On my way back to the stage, Philip popped out of Mr. Bateman's   90
art class, turned to the open door, and said, "**Eat it**, Tim."

"**Homo**," someone inside the door said. "**Queerbait**."

Philip **gave them two middle fingers**, and I ran up and **karate-kicked the door shut**.

"**Screw 'em**," he said.   95

"Screw 'em," I nodded.

65 pecked me on the lips:「唇に軽くキスをした」 身体への接触を表す表現は、「V + 人 + 身体の部位を表す副詞句」

69 mister:「そこの君」

71 steel-toed boots:「爪先に金属が入ったブーツ」

72 shop:「教材準備室」に相当する、教員用の部屋。

76-77 a varsity linebacker:「学校の代表チームのラインバッカー（アメリカン・フットボールのポジションの一つ）」

79-80 Mr. Lycker was none too happy about his son being in a play.

Q. 3 　理由を考えてみましょう。

83 college track: 大学進学を主眼としたコースのこと。

84 non-AP math: AP は Advanced Placement のことで、高校生による大学の授業の先取り履修のこと。non- が付いているので、このAPではない数学の授業を意味している。

85 woodshop:「木工の授業」

85-86 liked to stop me in the hall and give me his emptiest stare: あえて無関心を装うことで自分の権威を見せつけようとする教員（ライカー先生）に対するダンの皮肉な見方が表されている。

87 power :「権力」

91 Eat it:「くたばりやがれ」（激しい憎悪・悪意を表す罵りの表現）

92 Homo: 次のQueerbaitとともに男性同性愛者に対する差別的な表現。

93 gave them two middle fingers:「連中に両手の中指を立てて見せた」

93-94 karate-kicked the door shut:「空手のようなキックでドアを蹴って閉めた」

95 Screw 'em:「あいつらなんかくそくらえ」（'em = them）

Philip was a senior, and I only knew him through the play. His **cherubic** face was framed by long **whispy** hair, where a couple of **spit-wads** were caught, and he reached up to brush them away. Walking to the common area, he asked me if my brother had really choked out that kid last year, and I looked at my shoes and **sighed yes**.

"Man, I can imagine. There are times I could…" He **mimed** strangling someone.

"**Not like it got him anywhere**."

"Yeah," he said, and I could tell from the way he changed his voice he was **doing lines from the play**, though not his own. "That's what I **oughta** do—**bust on outa** here and nail the door shut behind."

"You **wouldn't** see Steven anymore."

"Oh, Steven," Philip put a hand over his chest and swooned against a **bank** of lockers. Once I'd been backstage, watching them run through the final scene, where Steven has to lift the AC unit and throw it through a **candy glass** window **Ms. C had paid for** out of her own pocket. Philip wasn't in the scene, and I felt him standing next to me watching Steven flex and heave as he hefted the unit. Under his breath, Philip said, "**So dreamy**."

(46)   Philip wasn't interested in girls and had memorized the soundtrack to **_The Rocky Horror Show_**. Anyone who was paying attention knew he was different, though no one talked about it. At best, he was ignored or politely tolerated, and at worst, well, the other kids gave him pretty a hard time. After he graduated, Philip would indeed "**bust out**," though he'd have **a tough run of it**: bad boyfriends and dead-end jobs. He'd eventually **straighten things out** and, to everyone's amazement, **wind up with** blue hair and a seat on the Seattle City Council. But back then no one imagined such things were possible for him.

When we got to the common room Philip walked into the **administrative office**, where he had **a standing invitation** to talk to the school counselor. I turned toward the stage and found Ms. C waiting with my brother.

98 cherubic:「天使のようにふっくらとした」

whispy :「細い房の」

98-99 spit-wads: 噛んで丸めた紙で、ストローで吹いて人に当てる。

101 sighed yes:「ため息をついて、そうだよと言った」

102 mimed:「〜の動作をしてみせた」

104 Not like it got him anywhere: = It's not like ...「それで何かがどうなるものでもないんだけど」

106 doing lines from the play:「劇の台詞を言う」

107 oughta: = ought to

bust on:「逃げ出す、抜け出す」

outa: = out of

108 wouldn't: 前の発言を受けて、ここからどこかへ行ってしまったら、という仮定のもとに、「(そんなことをしたら)スティーヴンに会えなくなるよ」という仮定法を表すのにwould が用いられている。

110 bank:「(ここではロッカーの)列」

112 candy glass: 割れても危なくない、ガラスにみせかけた小道具の「ガラス」。

Ms. C had paid for:「コセンティーノ先生が自腹を切って支払った」(windowのあとにthatを補って考える)

115 So dreamy:「夢みたい」(スティーヴンの頑強な肉体に魅力を感じていることを示す発言)

117 *The Rocky Horror Show*: イギリスのロック・ミュージカル (1973年)、およびそれにもとづいて製作された映画 (1975年)。映画にはとくに同性愛者のあいだでカルトムービーとして絶大な人気を誇った。

121 bust out:「爆発的な変化を遂げる」

122 a tough run of it: it は状況を示す。「変化の過程で辛い目にあう」

123 straighten things out:「いろいろなゴタゴタにきっちりカタをつけて」

123-124 wind up with:「結局…に落ち着く」

127 administrative office:「事務室」(スクール・カウンセラーのいるような相談室など、生徒に対応する部署を含む)

a standing invitation:「いつでも来てよいものとされている」

💬 **Expression**   本文を参考に次の表現を英語に直す時に空所に入る語を書きなさい。

1. 彼女は彼が体がこわばって階段から落ちたのを見た。

   She saw him (   ) stiff and fall down the stairs.

2. その内装が本当に家を古くさくみせている。

   The decor really (   ) the house.

3. 彼はすごくかっこよかった。

   He was completely (   ).

4. 象の群れを見た。

   I saw a (   ) of elephants.

5. 「続けて。」

   "(   ) on."

💡 **Comprehension**   次の問いに答えなさい。

1. which her parents had said would be much, much better for her. (ℓℓ.4-5) とありますが、ランダにとってよかったことは何だと両親は考えていましたか。

2. smelled like wet dogs, (ℓ.7) とは、どのような匂いの例えでしょうか。

3. not just annual performances of *A Christmas Carol.* (ℓℓ.15-16) からどのようなことがわかりますか。

4. コセンティーノ先生が決めた *One Flew Over the Cuckoo's Nest*『カッコーの巣の上で』の配役の特徴はどのようなものでしたか。

5. We'd fallen out of touch over the summer (ℓℓ.44-45) とは、どのようなことを指しますか。

6. Her eyes shined like marbles, (ℓℓ.59-60) はどうしてこうなったのですか。

_____

7. Philip gave them two middle fingers, (ℓ.93) の時のフィリップの気持ちはどのようなものでしたか。

_____

8. "Not like it got him anywhere." (ℓ.104) の言葉に込められた意味は何ですか。

_____

9. a tough run of it (ℓ.122) とは、なんのことでしょうか。

_____

10. フィリップについて no one imagined such things (ℓ.125) とありますが、どのようなことが想像できなかったのですか。

_____

⇄ **Discussion**

1. Her reasons were the same things I hated about it, (ℓℓ.38-39) の理由について、話し合ってみましょう。

_____

2. ライカー先生の人柄について、話し合ってみましょう。

_____

Unit: 6

✎ Writing

Write about one of your favorite movie stars and include the titles of the movies they've appeared in.

𝒢rammar 𝒢uide — 関係詞節の挿入（連鎖関係詞節）

which her parents had said would be much, much better for her (ℓℓ.4-5) では、her parents had said が挿入されています。先行詞は前文の内容を受けており、「その事自体は、彼女の両親が言っていたことだったが、彼女にとって良かったことではあった」となります。

One Flew East, One Flew West « 3 »

Unit : 7

前半では大学進学を考える時期にありながら勉強には興味が持てないロブの
様子が描かれます。後半では離婚して子供を育てるMs.C＝コセンティーノ先
生の苦労や政治への関心からアメリカ社会の問題を垣間見ることができます。

Pre-reading

1. アメリカの大学入試制度について調べてみましょう。

2. アメリカの医療保険制度について調べてみましょう。

3. *One Flew Over the Cuckoo's Nest*（『カッコーの巣の上で』）がなぜ上演題目として問題と
   なるのか、調べてみましょう。

Vocabulary

次の語の定義を下記のａからｊの中から選びなさい。

1. sophomore	**2.** tangle	**3.** relic	**4.** spurt	**5.** inflate
6. feral	**7.** shrug	**8.** banish	**9.** overwhelm	**10.** nod

a. an old object or custom that reminds people of the past or that has lived on from a past time

b. to raise and then lower your shoulders in order to show that you do not know something or do not care about something

c. to feel the emotion so strongly that they cannot think clearly

d. (American English) a student who is in their second year of study at a college or high school

e. to move your head up and down, especially in order to show agreement or understanding

f. (literary) to try to stop thinking about something or someone

g. short sudden increase of activity, effort, speed, or emotion

h. living wild, especially after escaping from life as a pet or on a farm

i. a twisted mass of something such as hair or thread

j. to make something larger by filling something

🎧 Disc 2 (1)

Rob had first period free, like all the sophomores, and was supposed to be studying for **the SAT**. But he wasn't interested in studying, and Ms. C had something else in mind.

"So, this is your brother?" she asked. Neither of us were sure who she was talking to, but we **locked eyes**. "I know we're a bit behind on ⁵ **prep** for tonight. We **could use** an extra pair of hands, and it'll be an **enriching** experience."

"I got it under control," I said. "Don't need any help."

"Now, Daniel. **I want you two to get along**. Give him something to do." 10

Ms. C rushed off, leaving him scowling at me. I took the stairs to the stage. "Come on."

The sheets on the hospital stretcher bed were still in a tangle from the dress rehearsal, so I had Rob help me make the bed. I tested the CD of **air raid sirens** and **nursery rhymes** over the sound system, and 15 he stood on the stage saying, louder, louder.

(2)   We needed to move the AC unit near the back of the stage, and I **brought out** the wheeled handcart, but Rob said it didn't look too heavy. The unit was half as tall as I was, a hundred-pound **relic from the cafeteria building**, which had been remodeled over the summer. I'd 20 cut off all the cords and tubes and **whitewashed** it, but you could see gray patches of metal showing through the paint. Ms. C had convinced Steven to audition for the Bromden part because he was tall, **had a stoic delivery**, and could lift the thing. Rob **had hit his growth spurt** and was about the same height as Steven, but as **a senior**, Steven had 25 the advantage of two years spent in the gym, pumping weights and **inflating** his legs and arms to new swollen proportions; **my brother could hide behind a lamp post if he stood sideways**. During rehearsals, I'd asked Ms. C if I should rip the old machinery out of the unit to make it lighter, but she liked it heavy: "When the audience sees Steven 30 lift it, they'll be able to **tell** he isn't acting."

(3)   I told Rob we'd use the handcart, but he ignored me and crouched

²　the SAT: アメリカの大学入学共通テスト。

⁵　locked eyes:「(ぼくたちの) 視線が絡み合った」

⁶　prep: < preparation.「準備」

　　could use:「あったら助かる」

⁷　enriching:「ためになる」

⁹　I want you two to get along:「あなたたちふたりに、お互い仲良くしてもらいたい」

¹⁵　air raid sirens:「空襲警報」

　　nursery rhymes:「(伝承の) 童謡」 芝居のタイトルは、この短編小説のタイトルとともに、"One flew east, one flew west, / One flew over the cuckoo's nest" で始まる童謡から取られている。

¹⁸　brought out:「持ってきた、持ち出した」

¹⁹⁻²⁰　relic from the cafeteria building: 文字どおり取れば、「カフェテリアの建物の遺跡」、つまりカフェテリアで使わなくなったエアコンをもらってきて芝居の小道具とした、ということ。

²¹　whitewashed:「白く塗り直した」

²³⁻²⁴　had a stoic delivery:「自分を抑えるような話し方をした」

²⁴　had hit his growth spurt:「急激な成長期をすでに迎えていた」

²⁵　a senior:「4年生」1行目の sophomore は2年生なので、その差は2年。

²⁷　inflating:「筋肉を (鍛え上げて) つける」

²⁷⁻²⁸　**Q.1** my brother could hide behind a lamp post if he stood sideways. とは、Rob の体格がどうだと言っているのでしょうか。

³¹　tell:「(見て) 分かる」

down, got his arms around the unit. He **tensed up** and threw all his strength **against it**, **lips straining away from his teeth** like a feral animal. The thing shifted, tilting to one side—but Rob **buckled under** 35 **the strain**, his grip slipped, and he landed on his butt on the stage. The unit fell back and thudded against the wooden floor.

I went over with the hand cart, slid the plate under the unit, tipped it back, and wheeled it to one corner of the stage. I came back and sat next to Rob, who was catching his breath. 40

"**Leave Lenny alone**," I said. "You guys used to be friends."

"Why? What'd he say to you?"

"He wasn't the one **messing with** Shanae."

"Oh, yeah? Who was it?"

I shrugged my shoulders and got to my feet. I didn't want to give 45 him somewhere else to direct his sullen anger. Sometimes I didn't even want to be related to him; I wished I lived in **a place where my name wouldn't have associated us**.

He said, "Your teacher asked if I was going to test prep for first period, wanted to know if I was **planning on** college. I think she couldn't 50 believe I was your brother."

(4) Even now I couldn't say **why Rob responded to our parents splitting up the way he did**—with a mean, unhappy look and **a get-lost attitude**—while I responded the way I did, **by feeling dull and depressed** for a year and burying myself in comics and books, reading 55 *Tortilla Flat* though I barely understood one thing it said in all its pages. I suppose, being **younger**, I hadn't yet grasped that the conflicts around us wouldn't always be resolved by adults **as if by divine intervention**; I'd simply wanted to ignore the problems in our family until **they** evaporated from my life. But without knowing why, on some 60 level, I admired my brother's anger, although I feared its uncontrollable **nature** and the problems it created.

The bell rang for the end of first period, and Rob got up and walked off the stage, heading I hoped, to his second-period class and

33   tensed up:「筋肉に力を入れた」

34   against it:「それを持ち上げようと」

> **Q. 2** ▷ lips straining away from his teeth とはどういう表情でしょう。次の like a feral animal（「野獣のような」）から推察してください。

35-36 buckled under the strain:「筋肉の緊張に耐えきれなくなった」

41   Leave Lenny alone:「レニーのことはほっときなよ」

43   messing with:「ちょっかいを出す」

47-48 a place where my name wouldn't have associated us:「名前を出してもロブと自分が周囲の人の頭のなかで結びつけて考えられないですむような場所」仮定法に注意。

50   planning on:「〜するつもりである」

52-53 why Rob responded to our parents splitting up the way he did: our parents splitting up は「我々の両親が別れたこと」で、our parents が動名詞 splitting の意味上の主語となっている。the way he did の did は responded の代動詞で、「ロブがしたような反応」となり、ダッシュのなかでその反応が具体的に示されている。

53-54 a get-lost attitude:「周囲に喧嘩を売るような態度」（get lost は「失せろ!」に当たるような悪口）

54-55 by feeling dull and depressed:「感情が鈍くなって、鬱になりながら」

56   *Tortilla Flat*: ジョン・スタインベック（John Steinbeck, 1902-1968）の小説。1935年出版。主人公の名前が Danny であるところから言及されていると思われる。

57 **Q. 3** ▷ younger とありますが、比較の対象となっているのは誰でしょうか。

58-59 as if by divine intervention:「まるで神様が仲介してくれるみたいに」

60 **Q. 4** ▷ they は何を指しますか。

62 **Q. 5** ▷ nature は、次のどちらでしょうか。
>   A. wild plants, animals, earth and the weather
>   B. quality

Unit: 7

not going to find Lenny or Nick or Shanae. There was no way to know ₆₅ though, so I banished him from my thoughts and **looked among the passing students for Randa**.

⑤ Julie spent first period on the phone with her **ex-mother-in-law, playing a kind of verbal Tetris** to try to **get her to discreetly pay** for half of ₇₀ Darren's asthma medication. When she'd been substituting last year, she'd put Darren on the State's **Child Health Plan**, but they didn't cover **his brand of inhaler** and she'd had to pay with her credit card. Now she was full time at Rainier and had switched to **the Public Employees Benefits Plan**, which was much better, though she was still paying the ₇₅ bills from last year. However, she didn't want her ex-husband to find out about her finances; for the past year, he'd been **angling for joint custody**, saying he could be a role model and help provide for Darren. She knew what he could provide: his rich, dentist-father's money and **a glimpse of what the beginnings of a drinking problem looked like**, ₈₀ though he denied it. **Only after** Darren's grandmother agreed to think it over, **did Julie hang up**.

⑥ Before lunch, she taught two periods of middle-school English and one of high-school French, trying to remember the lessons she'd used as a tutor in *L'Alliance française*, though really her mind was on ₈₅ the play. Philip was **on edge**, and she worried his energy would surprise and overwhelm the other cast members. They had a good group though, Randa was a star, and Julie was confident they would **pull together**.

When the bell rang, she went to the teacher's lounge to warm up a leftover **burrito** from her and Darren's weekly Sunday dinner at **El** ₉₀ **Sarape**. She was in the process of **dousing** it in hot sauce when Sue Hamlin, the main high school English teacher and a veteran of the **faculty**, sat next to her and told her she was planning on coming to the opening.

"I think it's great what you've done with drama. We haven't ₉₅ had anything like this **in years**. It's good for the kids to engage with

66-67 **looked among the passing students for Randa**: among the passing students をはさんで、looked for Randa となる。

69 **ex-mother-in-law**:「元・義理の母」つまり別れた夫の母親。

69-70 **playing a kind of verbal Tetris**: ビデオゲームの「テトリス」を引き合いにし、頭を使って相手と駆け引きをして「落とし所」を探ることを比喩的に表している。

70 **get her to discreetly pay**: 別れた夫の母親ではあるが、子ども（その女性にとっては孫）のぜんそくの薬代を相応に出してもらおうとしている。discreetly:「過不足なく適切と思われる金額になるように」

72 **Child Health Plan**:「（ワシントン州が提供している）子ども医療保険」

73 **his brand of inhaler**:「ダレンが使っているメーカーの吸入器」

74-75 **the Public Employees Benefits Plan**: 教員など公務員に対する保険制度のこと。

77-78 **angling for joint custody**:「共同後見人になろうと策略をめぐらせて」

80 **a glimpse of what the beginnings of a drinking problem looked like**:「アルコール中毒のはじまりがどんな様子であるかを垣間見せるような状態」

81-82 **Only after ... did Julie hang up**:「…したあとでようやく〜した」の形で、副詞節を前に出して強調しているので、主節が倒置となっている。

85 *L'Alliance française*:「アリアンス・フランセーズ（フランス政府公認の、フランス語・フランス文化普及のための非営利団体）」

86 **on edge**:「神経を尖らせている、ぎりぎりの」

88 **pull together**:「協調して働く」

90 **burrito**:「ブリート（具をトルティーヤでまいたメキシコ料理）」

90-91 **El Sarape**: オリンピアにあるメキシコ料理店。コセンティーノ先生はそこでの食べ残し（leftover）を持ち帰り、温め直してランチにしている。

91 **dousing**:「つける、つっこむ」

93 **faculty**:「（集合的に）教職員」

96 **in years**:「もう何年も」

controversial material."

⑺   Busy with rehearsals for the last month and a half, Julie hadn't been talking to the other teachers as much as she had in the days after she'd first started at the school. She had no idea what might be controversial about the play but nodded to Sue. John Lycker walked into the lounge, **making a beeline** for the coffee maker. 100

"You must be excited for Steven," Sue said to him.

He looked up. "Sure never expected he'd been in a play."

When she'd come upon the idea of casting the boy, Julie hadn't realized he was the son of the football coach. After finding out, she thought it was a **happy** coincidence: who wouldn't be glad to see their kid in a main role? But she hadn't known much about John at the time—he hardly spoke at the staff meetings—and now she wondered if she'd made a mistake. 105

She said to him, "Steven says he's looking forward to it. His teammates are all coming to see."

John filled his cup from the coffee pot and nodded. "Really?"

Sue said, "Years ago, a school **down in Aberdeen** tried to ban the book because of '**socialist influences**.' Parents were **up in arms**. I'm sure you won't have any problems though." 115

John looked at Sue and her. "People have to come to these things in their own time."

⑻   Having delivered this line, he exited through the doorway to the left. Sue rolled her eyes: "You know, I heard he told his students **Pat Buchanan** was the only one fit for the presidency." 120

On the back bumper of Sue's Subaru Outback, wedged between stickers imploring her fellow commuters to *Save our Schools* and *Keep it Green*, Julie **had spotted** the ***Clinton-Gore '96* logo**, which would surely be replaced by **a *Gore 2000* sticker at the earliest possible convenience**. After what had happened with **the protests up in Seattle**, Julie had **unplugged** from the news, and politics was **the last thing she wanted to talk about** during her lunch. She told Sue she needed to set 125

97 controversial:「議論を呼ぶような」

102 making a beeline for:「〜に向かってまっすぐに進んで」

107 **Q. 6》** happyは、次のどちらでしょう。

   A. fortunate and convenient

   B. feeling contentment

114 down in Aberdeen: このAberdeenはワシントン州西部の太平洋岸の都市を指す。down は通常は「南」の意味で用いることが多いが、この場合は「海のほう」「西のほう」を漠然と指す。

115 socialist influences: 虐げられているものたちが力を合わせて権力に立ち向かおうとする 内容が「社会主義的」と曲解されている。

 up in arms:「強い反対を示して」

121-122 Pat Buchanan: 1938年生まれ。極右の政治評論家、政治家。

125 had spotted:「すでに見つけていた」

 Clinton-Gore '96 logo: 1996年のアメリカ大統領選挙の際に民主党からの候補、ビル・ クリントン（副大統領アルバート・A・ゴア）を支持するロゴ。一般的に民主党のほうがリベ ラルとされる。

126 a *Gore 2000* sticker: 2000年に行われる選挙では民主党は上述のゴアを候補者として大 統領選を戦った。そのときの、民主党を支持することを示すステッカー。

126-127 at the earliest possible convenience:「都合がつき次第できるだけ早く」

127 the protests up in Seattle: 1999年11〜12月にかけてシアトルで行われたWHO閣僚会 議に際し、環境問題や反グローバリズムの立場から激しいデモが行われた。「シアトルの戦い」 と言われることもある、大規模な抗議行動だった。

128 unplugged:「つながりを断つ」（本来は「電源を抜く」の意）

128-129 the last thing she wanted to talk about:「いちばん話題にしたくないこと」

up the lighting for tonight and **excused herself**. 130

(9)   She brought her burrito backstage and **found me making sure** the costumes and wigs were hung up in the right order. As she later told me, to her I seemed shy, a bit of **lost soul**. In the morning, I'd often be out front, playing **hacky sack** with the **skaters** and **goth** kids, but **the way I combed my hair and dutifully wore the clothes my mom bought** 135 **me suggested I wasn't truly one of them**. She saw a painting I'd done in Harry Bateman's art class and decided to appoint me as set designer and stage manager. **It'd be a good use of my skills, and I might even make a friend or two**.

"Are we ready for tonight?" she asked me. "There's going to be a 140 crowd. **I need this to go well**."

130 **excused herself:** 「(失礼しますと言って)その場を去る」

131 **found me making sure:** このfoundには「見つける」の意味はほとんどない。「先生がブリートを持って舞台裏に来たとき、ぼくは…を確かめているところだった」となる。

133 **lost soul:** lostは「道に迷った」「どうしてよいか分からない」などの意。soulには「人」の意味があることから、全体で「集団に溶け込めない人」。

134 **hacky sack:** 「足で回すジャグル用の小さな皮のボール」

skaters: 「スケートボードで遊ぶ連中」

goth: 「ゴス系のファッションの」

134-135 **the way ... :** この文の主語はthe wayで、あとにin whichを補うと、I combed my hair ... and dutifully wore the clothes [my mom bought me] までが主部となる。the way ... suggested (that) I wasn't truly one of them. というのが文全体の構成。

136 **Q. 7** ▶▶ この文の最後の them が指すものは何でしょう。

138-139 **It'd be a good use ... :** この一文はいわゆる描出話法で、コセンティーノ先生が言った内容を表している。Itは前文の内容、つまり、「この劇で背景デザインと舞台の管理を担当すること」を指す。「この仕事は、あなたの腕の見せ所になるだろうし、ひょっとしたらひとりかふたり、友だちができるかもしれないよ」の意。

141 **I need this to go well:** 「今日の上演は、どうしても成功させたい」

Unit: 7

💬 **Expression** 本文を参考に次の表現を英語に直す時に空所に入る語を書きなさい。

1. 私はゆっくりと立ち上がった。

I (   ) to my feet.

2. "Lend me ten thousand yen." 「知るかよ。」

"(   ) lost."

3. 私は本を読むのに夢中だった。

I was burying (   ) in my books

4. その事件のせいで、彼らの戦略が少しは理解できた。

The incident provided a (   ) of their strategy.

5. 彼は神経を尖らせている。

His nerves are all on (   ).

💡 **Comprehension** 次の問いに答えなさい。

1. Rob had first period free, like all the sophomores, (ℓ.1) にあるようにどうして1時間目の授業を受けなくてもよかったのですか。

2. Ms. C had something else in mind. (ℓ.3) でコセンティーノ先生 (Ms. C) が考えていたことは何だと思われますか。

3. コセンティーノ先生が兄を連れてきた時の、「ぼく」の態度はどうでしたか。

4. ロブにエアコンのユニットを運んでもらおうとした時、結局どうなってしまいましたか。

5. playing a kind of verbal Tetris (ℓℓ.69-70) とは、どのようなことですか、説明しなさい。

6. and now she wondered if she'd made a mistake. (ll.109-110) とありますが、なぜ間違ったと思ったのですか。

7. ライカー先生がPat Buchananを大統領候補と考えているのはどうしてですか。

8. Julie had spotted the *Clinton-Gore '96* logo. (l.125) とあったステッカーはどのような新しいポスターに張り替えられると思いましたか。

9. politics was the last thing she wanted to talk about during her lunch (ll.128-129) とは、どのようなことを指しているのですか。

10. I seemed shy, a bit of lost soul. (l.133) とは、どのような感じだったのですか。

Unit: 7

⇄ Discussion

1. 両親が離婚した時の「ぼく（ダン）」とロブの行動の違いを話し合ってみましょう。

2. 69行目で、コセンティーノ先生(Ms. C)の呼称がJulieになっています。その意味を話し合ってみましょう。

✎ **Writing**

Write a short paragraph about your friends from your high school days.

Grammar Guide —— 使役動詞 have + 目的語 + 原形不定詞

I had Rob help me make the bed.（ℓ.14）の構文では前半部に使役動詞の had に目的語の Rob、原形不定詞の help（to のない不定詞で見た目は動詞の原形）でまず考え、「私はロブに手伝ってもらった」となります。help+人＋原形不定詞「人に…するのを手伝ってもらう」が続いて「私はロブにベッドメイキングを手伝ってもらった」の意味になります。

Unit: 8

いよいよ劇が上演される当日となりました。観客が集まり始め、離婚した「ぼく（ダン）」の両親もやって来ます。開演直前にMs. Cは生徒を励まし、観客に挨拶をするのでした。さて、上演はうまく行くのでしょうか。

📖 Pre-reading

1. これからどのような劇が上演されるのか、これまでの情報を整理してまとめましょう。

2. アメリカやイギリスの学校でどのようにドラマの授業が行われているか調べてみましょう。

🎙 Vocabulary

次の語の定義を下記のａからｊの中から選びなさい。

1. drift	**2.** bleachers	**3.** slat	**4.** twirl	**5.** grunt
6. psychiatric	**7.** collapse	**8.** petulant	**9.** frigid	**10.** groan

a. a thin flat piece of wood, plastic etc, used especially in furniture

b. to make short sounds or say a few words in a rough voice, when you do not want to talk

c. to suddenly fall down or become unconscious because you are ill or weak

d. not friendly or kind, very cold

e. to move, change, or do something without any plan or purpose

f. relating to the study and treatment of mental illness

g. to turn around and around or make something do this

h. behaving in an unreasonably impatient and angry way, like a child

i. a long deep sound that you make when you are in pain or do not want to do something

j. long wooden benches arranged in rows, where you sit to watch sport

Unit: 8

⑩ I watched through the curtain as people started arriving, paying their ten dollars to the members of the cast, who took turns standing by the door with a roll of paper tickets, a stack of programs, and **a fanny pack** filled with small bills to make change. Philip's **disoriented-looking** parents came in first, his dad in clean, stiff **flannel** and **a Stihl baseball cap**, Mrs. Lapman and Ms. Hamlin wandered over from their classrooms, then a few football-team boys arrived in a group, and Mr. Lycker after them. They all drifted toward the **bleachers**, which I'd pulled out and cleaned of the candy wrappers **kids sometimes shoved in** between the slats. Opposite the seats was the stage, and below it was an old mattress wrapped in a white sheet that would **break the fall** of the AC unit when Steven threw it.

⑪ I'd insisted Mom and Dad be at opening night, and they showed up within a few minutes of each other, **politely** exchanged hellos, and sat as far away from one another as they possibly could. My parents had given Rob ten **bucks** for a ticket, but I'd told him he could hang out in Ms. C's classroom and keep the cash if he stuck around for half an hour afterward and gave me a ride home.

Behind the curtain, Randa was in costume except for her beanie, which she twirled around one finger. Her lips moved but no sound came out and she paced behind the set wall, going over her lines a millionth time. Ms. C had left right after school to pick up her son, and now she swept back into her classroom **smelling like a campfire under a light layer of perfume**.

⑫ "We need more chairs. Darren, Daniel, **other Overton boy**, grab two each and take them out front."

Rob had been hunched over a paperback of ***Black Hawk Down***, but now he looked up and I set two chairs next to him. He just grunted but he picked them up, and the three of us marched into the common area, where the audience was gathering. Ms. C was right: at least a dozen more football players had showed up, along with Mr. Bateman and Principal Brown, and Randa's dad, who wore a dark suit with

⁴ a fanny pack:「ウェストポーチ」

⁵ disoriented-looking:「所在なげな様子で」

⁶ flannel:「ネルのシャツ」

a Stihl baseball cap:「（チェーンソーのメーカー）スティールのロゴがついた野球帽」このふたつから、林業関係の仕事ではないかと推測される。

⁹ bleachers:「観客席のベンチ」

¹⁰ kids sometimes shoved in:「生徒たちがときどき押し込む～」前の the candy wrappers を修飾している。

¹² break the fall:「落下のショックを和らげる」

¹⁴ politely:「社交的に」周囲に対して外見を取り繕っている様子。

¹⁶ bucks:（口語表現で）「ドル」

²³⁻²⁴ smelling like a campfire under a light layer of perfume:「軽くつけた香水の下から、キャンプファイアのような匂いを漂わせて」

²⁵ other Overton boy:「もうひとりのオーヴァートン君」 先生が、ロブの名前を思い出せなかったので、こういう表現で呼びかけた。

²⁷ *Black Hawk Down*: アメリカの作家マーク・ボウデン (Mark Bowden, 1951-) が書いたノンフィクション小説（1999年刊）。ソマリアにおけるアメリカ軍の作戦を描く。

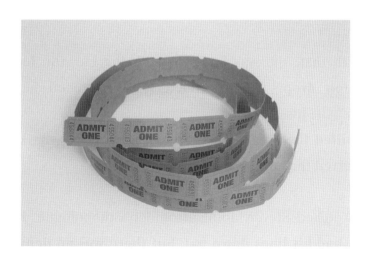

gold buttons and **looked like he might form these country people into an orchestra and begin conducting them right then and there**. The bleachers were full, and **we made two trips back for more chairs before we got everyone seated**. 35

(13)   Ms. C gathered the cast around the desk in her classroom and told them they'd worked hard, she had faith in them, and there was no turning back. "You're not here, at school. You're far in the future, you've grown into adults, and you're not even the same person you used 40 to be. **Make yourself believe that, and you'll dazzle them tonight**." Then she walked to the curtains and slipped out onto **the apron of the stage**. Standing in **the wings** by **the lighting panel**, I watched her from the side as she thanked the audience for coming and said how excited she was. 45

"I realize I'm new to this school, this community. Perhaps, I do things **a bit differently than** what you're used to, though I hope you can accept me." She clasped her hands, smiled, and moved her eyes across the audience. "However, tonight is **nothing to do with me, but** with the talents of your friends, your teammates, your children, and your 50 students. For weeks, they've given themselves to this **production**, really put everything they have into it, and I hope you're proud of them. I know I am."

With that, she was back through the curtain, **letting her calm expression drop**. A determined look tightened across her face. 55 "**Places**," she hissed.

I **killed the houselights**. Steven went to his mark, head bowed, and I parted the curtains.

(14) Philip watched Steven doing Bromden's monologue. He was nice to 60 look at, **had his lines down pat**, **but there was no denying it**: the boy was a bit dull. The energy of the audience—so many more people **than Philip** had ever seen at a drama club play—**threatened to overwhelm Steven** as he stood alone, talking to them **like** he was trying to **reason**

33-34 looked like he might form these country people into an orchestra and begin conducting them right then and there:「まるで、こういう田舎の人たちでオーケストラを編成して、まさにその場で指揮を始めようとするみたいに」

35-36 we made two trips back for more chairs before we got everyone seated:「あと2回、イスを取りに戻って、ようやく全員を座らせることができた」

41 Make yourself believe that, and you'll dazzle them tonight:「自分にそのこと（前の2文の内容）を信じ込ませなさい。そうしたら、今夜、あなたたちは観客が目を回すような演技ができる。」

42-43 the apron of the stage:「観客席に向かって舞台が張り出している部分、前舞台」

43 the wings:「舞台の袖」

the lighting panel:「照明装置のパネル」

47 a bit differently than:「…とは少々違ったふうに」 differentlyのあとはfromが正しいが、口語ではよくthanが用いられる。

49 nothing to do with me, but ... : not A, but B（AではなくてB）という熟語のヴァリエーション。「私のこととは関係なくて、今晩、関係あるのは…」の意。

51 production:「上演」

54-55 letting her calm expression drop:「冷静な表情がさっと変わって」

56 Places:「みんな、持ち場について」（舞台用語）

57 killed the houselights:「観客席の照明を落とした」

61 had his lines down pat:「自分のセリフをきちんと覚えてすらすら言える」 downは口語で「覚えている」、patは「すらすらと」の意。

but there was no denying it: itはコロンのあと、つまり「スティーヴンがあまり上手ではない」ことを指す。there is no denying は「〜は否定しようがない」

62-63 than Philip:「フィリップ以外にも」（ℓ.47の註も参照のこと）

63-64 threatened to overwhelm Steven: 観客の無言の圧力が凄くて、スティーヴンがたじたじとなっている様子を示している。

64 like:（口語で）「まるで…しようとしているかのように」（= as if）

64-65 reason with:「を説得する」

with a silent, furious mob. The first minute dragged on, but soon the 65
actors playing the **orderlies** joined him, and then Philip made his
entrance. He added his own voltage to **the mix**, straining to **equalize**
the electricity onstage with **that** of the crowd.

It was a relief when Randa **came on**, her **booming** voice, her
swagger pushing back against the glow of the eyeballs staring at them. 70
Her energy calmed Philip, **allowed him to channel his excitement into**
the narrow strictures of his Dr. Ratched. Everything slowed and he
came to terms with the performance. It was brilliant.

(15)   He could feel it in the way the audience's attention focused and they
stopped **shifting** in their seats. No one got up to use the bathroom or 75
check their cell phone. They didn't even cough. In the final scene of the
first act, Randa as McMurphy began announcing a World Series game,
making up the plays and **calling them out** like a broadcast announcer,
even though Philip as Dr. Ratched had cut the power to the TV. At the
climactic line, all the patients of the psychiatric hospital leaped into 80
the air—"Home run!"—but Randa **came down awkwardly and fell**,
her back slamming against the floorboards.

Philip **projected an air of icy calm**, though a gleam of sweat shone
on his forehead. **A moment of silence** passed like a hard lump in the
throat. **A sneeze echoed out in the audience, the sound of someone** 85
crumpling their program. But Steven, sweet-beautiful Steven, with his
magnificent **burly** arms, **reached down and hauled her back up**, and
Lenny as Harding **led the cast of patients in a cheer**.

When I closed the curtains, Philip collapsed in relief. During
intermission, I went around, checking on each actor. I took Philip a 90
bottle of water, and he looked at me. "It's great, isn't it?"

Randa appeared next to me, taking the other bottled water I was
holding: "**It is**. It really is."

"**I want you meaner**. Cold, cold," Ms. C said to Philip from the
backstage doorway. She **pointed to Randa**: "Don't worry about the 95
fall. I liked your jump. **Keep up the physicality**."

66　orderlies:「(病院の)雑役係」

67　the mix:「(人の)集まり」ここでは舞台上の役者たち全体を指す。

　　equalize:「同じくらいにする」

68　that: = the electricity

69　came on:「舞台に登場した」

　　booming:「力のこもった」

70　swagger:「堂々とした歩きかた」

　　pushing back against:「〜に抵抗する」

71　allowed him to: 構文としては「彼に〜することを許す」であるが、「…のおかげで、彼は〜できるようになった」と考える。「ランダのエネルギーのおかげで、〜できるようになった」

71-72　channel A into B :「Aを変換してBへと注ぎ込む」自分の高揚感を台詞を言うことに向けて集中する、の意。

72　the narrow strictures of his Dr. Ratched: 前註の台詞の内容を示す。「自分の役であるラチェッド医師が述べる厳しい非難」

73　came to terms with the performance:「芝居(舞台の上の空気感)に溶け込んだ」

75　shifting:「もぞもぞ動くこと」

78　making up the plays:「(架空の)試合を即興ででっち上げて」

　　calling them out: themは直前のplays(試合の進行)を指す。

80　climactic line:「クライマックスの台詞」

81　came down awkwardly and fell:「(野球の試合の実況をするために上がっていた高いところから)よろよろと降りてきて、転んだ」

83　projected an air of icy calm:「氷のように冷静だという風を装った」

84　A moment of silence: ランダが倒れてシーンとなった、ということ。ランダの動作がアクシデントであったことを示している。

85-86　A sneeze ... : 突然の成り行きで、観客もどのように反応してよいか戸惑っている様子を表している。

87　burly:「たくましい」

　　reached down and hauled her back up:「ランダを抱えると、放り上げて元のところに戻した」 haul ... backで「投げて戻す」の意、upが物理的に上のほうであることを示している。

88　led the cast of patients in a cheer:「患者役のキャストを促して歓声を上げさせた」

93　**Q.1** It is. のあとに省略されているのはどういう単語でしょうか。

94　I want you meaner:「もっと嫌な奴のように演じなさい」

95　pointed to Randa:「ランダに向かって言った」

96　Keep up the physicality:「身体全体を使って表現することをその調子で続けなさい」

Unit: 8

(16)   The intermission **blinked by**, and then I was raising the curtain on the second act. For a moment, here and there, Philip and the rest of the main cast seemed to forget about the audience. They were growing in their roles, **filling out each corner of their characters**. Randa 100 was **all petulant**, **straight-jacketed energy**, while Philip had a frigid determination, which concealed a hidden resentment; the orderlies were **surly** workers, and the nurses were **sour automatons**.

It wasn't until well into the second act that it started to go wrong. In the fight scene, Bromden **was pulling one of the orderlies off McMurphy**, 105 but this supporting actor **had taken too much inspiration from Randa's performance**. He fought Steven's grip too enthusiastically, and the two of them **went down in a heap** on the stage as the lights went out. A groan of pain went up in the dark, **followed by a muffled dragging and another cry**. A light turned on backstage, **someone cursed**, and then a 110 door slammed. The light disappeared.

97　blinked by:「またたくまに過ぎた」

100　filling out each corner of their characters:「自分の役を隅々まで演じきって」

101　all petulant:「不機嫌さそのもの」

　　　straight-jacketed energy:「拘束衣を着せられたように行き場のないエネルギー」

103　surly:「不機嫌な、無愛想な」

　　　sour automatons:「悪意を持った機械人形（のような人）」

104　It wasn't until well into the second act that it started to go wrong:「様子がおかしくなりはじめたのは、第2幕が進んでだいぶん経ったころだった」

105　was pulling one of the orderlies off McMurphy:「マックマーフィともみ合っている雑役係のひとりを引きはがそうとしていた」

106-107　had taken too much inspiration from Randa's performance:「ランダの演技に感化されすぎてしまっていて」

108　went down in a heap:「もつれあったまま、ドサッと倒れた」

109-110　followed by a muffled dragging and another cry:「続いて、押し殺したようなうめき声がなかなかやまなかったが、さらにほかの叫び声も聞こえた」

110　someone cursed:「誰かが毒づいた」

💬 **Expression**　　本文を参考に次の表現を英語に直す時に空所に入る語を書きなさい。

1. 彼らは誰もがパーティに来るべきだと言い張りました。

They insisted that everyone (　　　　　　) come to the party.

2. 私はよく図書館に足を運んだものだった。

I used to make several (　　　　　　) to the library.

3. もう後戻りはできない。

There is (　　　　　) (　　　　　　) back.

4. 彼は父の死を受け入れようとはしなかった。

He never came to (　　　　　　) with his father's death.

5. 彼はホッとして安堵のため息をついた。

He finally sighed in (　　　　　).

💡 **Comprehension**　　次の問いに答えなさい。

1. small bills to make change (ℓ.4) とは、具体的に何のことですか。

2. フィリップの父の様子、stiff flannel and a Stihl baseball cap, (ℓ.6) からわかることはなんですか。

3. smelling like a campfire under a light layer of perfume (ℓℓ.23-24) とは、どのような様子を表現したのですか。

4. though I hope you can accept me. (ℓℓ.47-48) と言った時のコセンティーノ先生の気持ちを説明しなさい。

5. really put everything they have into it (ℓℓ.51-52) とは、どのようなことですか、説明しなさい。

6. He added his own voltage to the mix, straining to equalize the electricity onstage with that of the crowd. (ll.67-68) とは、どのようなことを表していますか。

_____

7. At the climactic line (ll.79-80) で起きたことを説明しなさい。

_____

8. "Keep up the physicality." (l.96) のこの場面での意味は何でしょうか。

_____

9. It wasn't until well into the second act that it started to go wrong. (l.104) とは、具体的にどのようなことが起きたのでしょうか、説明しなさい。

_____

10. this supporting actor had taken too much inspiration from Randa's performance. (ll.106-107) とは、どのようなことが起きたのですか。

_____

Unit: 8

⇄ **Discussion**

1. 劇が始まり、スティーヴンの演技がどう変化していったか、話し合ってみましょう。

_____

2. 第1幕と第2幕の違いを話し合ってみましょう。

_____

✏ Writing

If you played a role in a play, what would you do on the stage?

🚩 *Grammar Guide* — 副詞句の前置による強調と倒置

Opposite the seats was the stage, and below it was an old mattress ... (ℓℓ.10-12)の構文では、副詞句のopposite the seats が強調のために前置され、そのために動詞のwas が主語のthe stageの前に倒置されています。強調されたことを考慮に入れて、訳を考えると「席の反対側に舞台があった」の意味になります。通常の語順では、The stage was opposite the seats.「舞台は席の反対側にあった」です。そして、andの等位接続詞は同じ構造の文を並列させますから、副詞句のbelow it も同様に強調のために前置されたと考えられます。主語のan old mattressと動詞のwasが倒置され、「その下に古いマットがあった」の意味になります。通常の語順ではAn old mattress was below it.「古いマットがその下にあった。」となります。

Unit : 9

上演中にまさかのアクシデントが起こりますが、コセンティーノ先生の指示のもと出演者たちが何とか対処します。ロブに対する「ぼく(ダン)」の気持ち、ランダとの関係、そして、その後のコセンティーノ先生の人生が描かれます。

Pre-reading

1. アメリカの national anthem について調べてみましょう。

2. 『カッコーの巣の上で』で言及されたロボトミー手術とは何か、調べてみましょう。

Vocabulary

次の語の定義を下記のaからjの中から選びなさい。

1. crouch	**2.** limp	**3.** deliver	**4.** corpse	**5.** imperceptible
6. jerk	**7.** heave	**8.** improvise	**9.** custody	**10.** disperse

a. to walk slowly and with difficulty because one leg is hurt or injured

b. the dead body of a person

c. to pull or lift something very heavy with one great effort

d. almost impossible to see or notice

e. the right to take care of a child, given to their parents when they have divorced

f. to lower your body close to the ground by bending your knees completely

g. to invent music, words, a statement etc. from your imagination, rather than planning or preparing it first

h. to go away in different directions

i. to present (a speech, statement, etc.) to a group of people

j. to move with a quick sudden movement, or to make part of your body move in this way

(17) I **found** Ms. C crouched at the bottom of the backstage stairs, where Steven sat, **reaching for** his ankle. "**Damn**, I think—"

She **shushed** him and motioned for me to close the door. "What happened? Is it broken?"

"I **rolled it**. Rolled it bad."

"Can you go back out there?" I asked. "Next is the shock therapy scene."

"I can't put any weight on **it**."

Ms. C said, "You're sitting down in the next scene. We'll keep you out of the party scene."

"What about the last scene?" He asked. "I can't lift anything like this."

She told him **they'd figure it out**. I helped him get up and limp over to the rear wall of the set. In the total dark, he **hobbled** to the bench onstage and sat next to Randa. During the scene, Steven skipped over a couple of lines, but no one noticed. After the next scene, Ms. C told one of the orderly actors to go on stage and **pretend like he was picking up the room**. "Hum the national anthem. Hum slow. **Buy us some time**."

(18) The cast gathered in her classroom, and she told them about Steven's ankle injury. He only had a few lines in the next scene, the party, and they could **improvise** without him. "The problem is the last scene. Bromden gives his monologue, **smothers** Randall, throws the unit through the window."

I said, "He just stands there most of the time. Steven can do the monologue from backstage. You could even cut out his final lines of dialogue. If someone switches costumes with him, they could **face away from the audience** for most the scene."

Ms. C shook her head, "Who's going to lift the air-conditioning unit? It's too heavy."

"I can." Rob had put away his book and stood behind Lenny, apart

1 I found: このような find の用法については、Unit 7 131行目の註参照。

2 reaching for:「〜に手を伸ばしながら」

Damn:「ちくしょう！」などの罵り言葉。

4 shushed:「シッと静かにさせた」

6 rolled it:「ひねった」

9 **Q.1** it が指すものは、次のどれでしょう。

    A. scene

    B. ankle

14 they'd figure it out:「みんなで何とかする」

15 hobbled:「傷む足をかばってよたよた歩いた」

18-19 pretend like he was picking up the room:「部屋を片づけているふりをする」

19-20 Buy us some time:「（何か策を考えるまでの）時間稼ぎをして」

23 improvise:「即興で演技する」

24 smothers:「窒息死させる」

28-29 face away from the audience:「観客の目をそらす」

from the cast. "I can lift it."

"**There's got to be a better a way**," I said. "A cable?"

"He's on the team with me," Steven said. "**I bet he could**." 35

Rob shrugged. "If you need someone."

Ms. C said to Steven, "Give him your costume."

While Rob was **changing**, I said, "What are you doing?"

He didn't reply but slipped the hospital pajamas over his clothes. Even wearing Steven's costume, Rob didn't resemble him, but if he 40 kept his back to the audience for most of the scene, it would be hard to tell. I told him to stand still. "Then when you move, **be like a statue coming to life**. Take the pillow, hold it over Randa's head. She'll be able to breathe if you don't press down too hard."

(19)   After the party scene, I blacked out the lights, **walked** Rob over 45 to the mark where he needed to stand, and made sure he was **facing upstage**. Steven sat in a chair **inside the doorway that led onto the stage** and delivered his monologue into the darkness. Once he finished, the other actors made their entrances, and I brought up the lights.

Halfway through the scene, the other actors exited, and Rob was 50 alone with Randa as McMurphy, lying **lobotomized** in the hospital bed. A long moment passed, another, but Rob didn't move. **He'd seized up**.

Finally, **an imperceptible shift of his shoulders, and** he began **shuffling over to the bed**, his head down. Slow, slow, he took the pillow from atop Randa's legs and began to smother **her character** with it. She 55 **jerked and thrashed, acting out her death throes**, and then went limp. Lenny came on as Harding and pulled Rob away from the corpse. He wept over Randa and delivered his line, "Go. **Beat it out of here!**"

(20)   His back to the audience, Rob went over to the old AC unit. He walked behind it, squatted down, and got his arms around it. He 60 heaved, and it tilted like before, but it didn't **lift off the ground**. I heard the breath go out of him as he **let go**. He tried again, **straining against the bulk**, and when this failed, he stood up and looked down at it like an opponent he was **bent on conquering**. If the audience hadn't seen

34 There's got to be a better a way: 「もっと良い方法があるはずだ」

35 I bet he could: 「こいつならきっとやれるに違いない」

38 changing: 「着替えをする」

42-43 be like a statue coming to life: 「彫像が命を吹き込まれたようにするんだ」命令文。

45 walked: 「（歩いて）連れて行った」

46-47 facing upstage: 「舞台後方を向いて」

47-48 inside the doorway that led onto the stage: 「舞台に向かうドアの内側」

51 lobotomized: 「ロボトミー手術（前頭葉の外科手術。現在は行われない）を受けて」

52 He'd seized up: 「ロブは動けなくなってしまっていた」

53 an imperceptible shift of his shoulders, and ... : 「分からないくらい少しずつ肩を揺らすと〜」

54 shuffling over to the bed: 「ベッドのほうへのろのろと歩いて行った」

55 her character: ランダが演じているマックマーフィという役のこと。

56 jerked and thrashed: 「（断末魔で）身体を激しくばたばたさせた」

acting out her death throes: 「死ぬ間際の苦しみを演じて」

58 Beat it out of here!: 「ここからさっさと消え失せろ」

61 lift off the ground: 「床から持ち上がる」

62 let go: 「手を離した」

62-63 straining against the bulk: 「その重量物を持ち上げようと力を振り絞って」

64 bent on conquering: 「打ち負かそうと決意した」

him fully before, they did now. It didn't matter though. They were ₆₅
interested in this struggle, **the way** his face went red and the veins
stood out on his neck when he tried a third time. He released his grip,
fell across the top of the unit, and expelled **a defeated breath**.

(21)   I'd known this would happen and cursed myself: I'd instinctively
believed in him with **the blind faith of a younger brother**. "Just leave," ₇₀
I whispered, **looking away**. "Get off the stage."

     A ticking sound came from where he was. When I looked up, he
was **rocking the unit back and forth**. More, a little more.

     Lenny **improvised a line**: "**That's the way!**"

     Rob pushed it again, and again, until the thing seemed about to tip ₇₅
over. Then, **when it rocked back toward him, he crouched down and
pushed up against** it in one smooth motion. The unit fell against him,
and he struggled forward with a roar, trying to lift it from below. It was
still too heavy—he was going to lose it—but Lenny came over and
pushed from the opposite direction, **until it balanced on his shoulder**. ₈₀

     Rob took a staggering step, and **a smattering of applause** rang out
from the crowd, and I repented my doubt. He **waddled** forward under
the weight, right up to the edge of the stage, where the windowpane
hung from the **rafters**. He heaved, **chucking the unit off the stage**,
and the metal shattered the candy glass and crashed onto the mattress ₈₅
below. **For the first time in so long**, I was filled with pride in my brother
as I watched him dash down the stage stairs, making his escape.

(22) At the curtain call, Steven limped to the front of the stage, one arm
over Rob's shoulder and the other over Lenny's, and they all took a ₉₀
bow together. Later, Mom told me Rob smiled like she hadn't seen
him smile in months, a year maybe. **For three more performances**,
Rob would fill the role of Mr. Bromden in the final scene, while Steven
delivered his monologue from backstage.

     From the wings, Ms. C watched with her son as Philip came ₉₅
forward with the actors who had played his orderlies and nurses. She

66　the way: 直前の this struggle とカンマで同格につながれていると考えるとよい。

68　fell across the top of the unit: 「エアコンの上に倒れ込んだ」

　　a defeated breath: 「負けを認めるようなため息」

70　believed in him: 「ロブならやってのけるだろうと信じていた」
　　the blind faith of a younger brother: 「弟として、根拠がなくても兄の力を信じる気持ち」
　　不定冠詞は一般のものを指すので、弟とはそういうものだ、という感じが出ている。

71　looking away: 「顔をそむけて」 前項で述べた期待が裏切られた気持ちが出ている。

73　rocking the unit back and forth: 「エアコンを前後に揺らして」

74　improvised a line: 「台詞をアドリブで言った」

　　That's the way!: 「その調子だ！」

76　when it rocked back toward him: 「（向こうに押した反動で）ロブのほうに揺れて倒れかかってきたとき」

76-77　he crouched down and pushed up against it: 「しゃがみこんで下から支えた」

80　until it balanced on his shoulder: 「ついにエアコンはロブの肩のうえにバランスを取りながら乗っかった」

81　a smattering of applause: 「まばらな拍手」

82　waddled: 「ふらふら歩いた」

84　rafters: 「横木」

　　chucking the unit off the stage: 「エアコンを舞台から放り投げて」

86　For the first time in so long: 「これまで長い間感じていなかったが」

92　For three more performances: 「その後、3回の上演で」

Unit : 9

clapped louder than any of the parents and reached down to squeeze Darren's shoulder.

She was the best drama director Rainier High School ever had and an amazing teacher, one of the few who left her fingerprints on my life —when Mr. Suden did in fact retire before the next school year, **Principal Brown and the administration rewarded her by choosing not to give her a new contract. She was too good for them**, and they let her go without a second thought. For the next few years, she would go back to **substituting** at half a dozen of the worst schools in the State, and eventually, when her commute became too long and she took a night job waitressing **to make ends meet**, she had to agree to joint custody with her ex-husband.

Standing in the darkness, watching her actors soak in the applause, she didn't know any of this. She was happy, and the only **quibble** nagging her mind was the absence of Randa, who'd disappeared after the last scene. After I'd pulled the curtain closed on the final act, Randa had found me. She'd taken my hand and pulled me into the senior hallway outside Ms. C's classroom. She led me to one of **the recessed doorways**, a nook where she took me in her arms, enveloping me in **the fresh-bread smell of the sweat she'd worked up onstage**.

Her hands were magnets pulling me forward, and, in between, her breath brushed my cheek, my neck, the whorls of my ear. Her laughter was a story I'd known but forgotten; it said **how, every second, in the night sky, new galaxies burst into being**, and someday my atoms would disperse over the universe, go everywhere, anywhere. For the moment though, it reminded me, this was **where I was wanted**.

102-103 Principal Brown ... a new contract: 演劇の先生として優れていたが、校長と学校当局はコセンティーノ先生の契約を更新しない選択をする、という形で報いた。

103 She was too good for them, : 描出話法。「この先生は、うちのような学校に置いておくのはもったいない」というのが言い分であるが、とってつけたような口実に過ぎない。

105 substituting:「代用教員の仕事をする」Unit 5 18行目 の註を参照。

107 to make ends meet:「生活をやりくりしていくために」

110 quibble:「ささいな問題」

114-115 the recessed doorways:「ドアが壁から少し引っ込んでいる場所」

116 the fresh-bread smell of the sweat she'd worked up onstage:「ランダが舞台で演技することでかいた汗の、焼きたてのパンのような匂い」

119-120 how, every second, in the night sky, new galaxies burst into being: every second と in the night sky は挿入句なので、how new galaxies burst into being とつながる。「新しい銀河がどのようにして爆発して誕生するか」

122 where I was wanted:「ぼくが求められている所」I wanted ではないことに注意。

💬 **Expression**　本文を参考に次の表現を英語に直す時に空所に入る語を書きなさい。

1. 私の家族は太る体質である。

   My family has an inclination to (　　　　　　) on weight.

2. 私は部屋を片付けているふりをした。

   I pretended like I was (　　　　　　) up the room.

3. 彼は口実をつけて時間を稼ごうとした。

   He tried to (　　　　　　) time by giving many excuses.

4. 絨毯からホコリをたたき出しなさい。

   (　　　　　　) the dust of rugs.

5. その弁護士は彼の無罪を明らかにしようと決心した。

   The lawyer was (　　　　　　) on proving that he was innocent.

💡 **Comprehension**　次の問いに答えなさい。

1. "I rolled it. Rolled it bad." (ℓ.6) とは、どのような様子のことですか。

2. "I bet he could." (ℓ.35) のcouldのあとに続く表現を補い、なぜこのようなセリフを言ったのか、説明しなさい。

3. but Rob didn't move. He'd seized up. (ℓ.52) はどのような状況だったのでしょうか。

4. I heard the breath go out of him as he let go. (ℓℓ.61-62) からどのようなことがわかるでしょうか。

5. I'd known this would happen and cursed myself: (ℓ.69) のthis は何を指しているか明らかにしてこの文の意味を説明しなさい。

6. More, a little more. (ℓ.73) は、どのような状態を表しているでしょうか。

7. I repented my doubt. (ℓ.82) とは、どのような疑いだったのですか。

8. Mom told me Rob smiled like she hadn't seen him smile in months, a year maybe. (ℓℓ.91-92) からわかったことは何でしょうか。

9. the only quibble nagging her mind was the absence of Randa, who'd disappeared after the last scene. (ℓℓ.110-112) では、なぜランダが最終シーンの後で消えてしまったのですか。

10. it said how, every second, in the night sky, new galaxies burst into being, and someday my atoms would disperse over the universe, go everywhere, anywhere. (ℓℓ.119-121) で、彼女の笑いで、ダンはどのようなことを感じましたか。

Unit: 9

⇄ Discussion

1. I'd instinctively believed in him with the blind faith of a younger brother. (ℓℓ.69-70) とありますが、このときの兄に対する思いを話し合ってみましょう。

2. コセンティーノ先生のその後についてどうなったのかまとめてみましょう。また、彼女の後半生が幸せだったのかも考えてみましょう。

✐ Writing

What do you think about taking part in a school drama? Would you like to take part in a play? Why or why not?

Grammar Guide —— 未来のことを考える would

For three more performances, Rob would fill the role of Mr. Bromden in the final scene, (ℓℓ.92-93) の would は、過去時制の物語の中でこれから起きることを考えている場合に用いられます。「その後3回の上演で、ロブは最終幕のブロムデンさんの役をうまく果たせるでしょう」の意味です。would には仮定法や時制の一致、過去の習慣など様々な場面で用いられるので間違えないように気をつけましょう。

Chapter 3

Reunion

(24) The final story of the text is set in the early 2000s, when the United States had embarked on the global War on Terror and the Bush administration launched an invasion of Iraq, which would cost hundreds of thousands of lives before it was over. This conflict left deep scars on so many lives and is still little understood to this day.

In this case, the piece is set in Seattle, at the end of summer, when crowds of tourists flock to the piers and the Pike Place Market, roaming down to Pioneer Square and even the industrial areas of the Stadium District. Although it is not a sprawling metropolis, for people from the rural areas of Washington State, Seattle is "the big city," with all the implications of excitement, opportunity, and also danger that such a phrase implies. Through the protagonist's eyes, we see glimpses of the city's problems, especially the inequality and rampant homelessness, which would come to plague the city in the future decades.

The structure returns to a more straightforward style, although the narration reflects the fact that the protagonist has grown older. But is he any more enlightened, any wiser for these years?

　このテクストの最後の話の舞台は2000年代初頭です。当時、合衆国は世界的な対テロ戦争へと乗り出し、ブッシュ政権はイラク侵攻を開始しましたが、戦争が終わるまでに何十万もの命が失われることになりました。この衝突は多くの人々の生活に深い傷跡を残しましたが、それは今日でもほとんど理解されていません。

　今回、作品の舞台は夏の終りのシアトルです。大勢の観光客が桟橋やパイク・プレース・マーケットに押し寄せ、パイオニア・スクエアや球場地区周辺の工業地区までぶらつき歩いていました。シアトルは郊外にまで広がっていくような大都市ではありませんでしたが、ワシントン州の田舎からやってきた人々にとっては唯一の「大都会」で、そのような言葉が暗に意味するような興奮や機会や危険を伴う場所でした。われわれは、特に不平等や根深いホームレスの問題など、その後数十年間シアトルを悩ますことになる都市の問題を、主人公の目を通して垣間見ることができます。

　作品構造はよりストレートな形式に戻りますが、語りは主人公が成長したという事実を反映しています。しかし、この年月の間に、はたして彼は、より知識を得てより賢くなっているのでしょうか。

Unit: 10

「ぼく（ダン）」と兄ロブの物語は数年後の再会の場面へ移ります。家族構成もお互いの環境も大きく変わっています。

Pre-reading

1. シアトルはどのような街なのか、調べてみましょう。

2. creative writing の授業とはどのようなものか、調べてみましょう。

Vocabulary

次の語の定義を下記の a から j の中から選びなさい。

1. cavernous	**2.** register	**3.** glimpse	**4.** sodden	**5.** fare
6. adrift	**7.** commission	**8.** resume	**9.** grin	**10.** piece

a. to put someone's name on an official list

b. to start doing something again after stopping

c. very wet and heavy

d. to smile widely

e. a quick look at someone or something that does not allow you to see them clearly

f. something that has been produced by an artist, musician, or writer

g. to formally ask someone to write an official report, produce a work of art for you etc.

h. the price you pay to travel somewhere by bus, train, plane etc.

i. very large and deep

j. confused about what to do

(25) Getting off the train, I hurried through the Sunday crowd in the **cavernous** waiting room and came out into the industrial district. My vision **was charged with** nervous energy, and the **graffitied** warehouse buildings shone in the late afternoon, as if a rainstorm had passed and then the sun had broken through the clouds. 5

Dad had **dropped me off** at the **one-room train station** in Olympia earlier that day. Before I got out of the car, he **reached over** and put a hand on my arm.

"Don't worry," he said, **giving my shoulder a squeeze**. "You'll do fine. You and Rob look after each other." 10

I heard **a false note** in his encouragement, which **underlined my own disquiet**. The previous winter, I'd **bombed** my final exams and nearly **flunked out** of university. I **temporarily withdrew** and spent three **quarters waiting tables** and trying to decide if I should change my major. I'd **reenrolled** for the autumn quarter but hadn't registered 15 for classes yet and didn't know if I could stay focused or keep my grades up. My brother had moved to Seattle, and **I'd** stay with him for a few days before **heading to** campus.

(26) Despite my doubts, I hoped Dad was right as I walked to the bus stop, glimpsing the massive roof of **Safeco Field** in the distance. 20 **They'd built the baseball stadium on a vision of redevelopment and urban renewal, but the sodden tents of the homeless on the sidewalk gave the lie to these promises**, and I **steered a wide arc** around them. The City Center bus came **wheezing** up to the curb on the other side of the street as the walk signal turned to a flashing **red hand**—I dashed 25 in front of three lanes of traffic and squeezed on board just before the doors folded shut.

(27) "Get on. Hurry up. **My bus going anywhere, everywhere you want to go**." The driver shifted into gear, while I paid my money into the fare machine and **stumbled** into the back. 30

Between **tuition** and renting an apartment in the **U District**, my **savings** were down to the twenty-dollar bill **wedged** into my wallet next

2 cavernous:「洞窟のような」

3 was charged with:「(感情などが) みなぎった」

4 graffitied:「(壁などに) 落書きされた」

6 dropped me off:「(車で人を送り届けて) 降ろした」

one-room train station:「(駅舎が) 一部屋の小さな列車の駅」

7 reached over:「手を伸ばした」

9 giving my shoulder a squeeze:「肩をぎゅっとつかむ」

11 **Q. 1** 〉〉 a false noteとはどのようなことを指しているのか考え、文章全体の意味を考えてみましょう。

11-12 underlined my own disquiet:「私自身の不安を強めた」

12 bombed:「試験で落第した」

13 flunked out:「(成績不良で) 退学した」

temporarily withdrew:「一時的に (大学を) やめた ＝ 休学した」

14 quarters:「(1年4学期制の) 学期」

waiting tables:「ウェイターとして働き」

15 reenrolled:「(大学に) 復学した」

17 I'd: I wouldの省略形。

18 heading to:「〜へ向かう」

20 Safeco Field: ワシントン州シアトル市の野球場。メジャーリーグのシアトル・マリナーズの本拠地。現在はT-Mobile Parkに名称変更。

21-23 **Q. 2** 〉〉 この野球場周辺の描写はアメリカのどのような問題を表しているか考えてみましょう。

23 steered a wide arc:「遠巻きに迂回した」

24 wheezing:「ぜいぜいと言う音をたてて (バスが止まる音を表現)」

25 red hand:「(歩行者用信号の) 止まれのサイン」

28-29 My bus going anywhere, everywhere you want to go: 運転手の冗談めかしたアナウンスメント。

30 stumbled:「よろめいた」

31 tuition:「学費」

U District: シアトルのワシントン大学周辺の地区 (University District) の通称。

32 savings:「所持金」

wedged:「押し込んだ、差し込んだ」

to a check for **three hundred bucks** from my mom, though I couldn't **cash** it until the banks opened on Monday. I needed to live within my **means**. This was what Mom had told me when she handed me the check, saying **discipline was exactly what the Army had given Rob**. After getting his degree from **Washington State**, he'd also been adrift, living in a **grimy off-campus** house and working as a **bouncer**. Eventually, he signed up with the **Reserves**, and Mom flew to South Carolina to watch him graduate from **Basic Training**. Afterward, he found a job in Seattle, where he worked as a **paralegal** and trained with his **unit** one weekend a month. That Sunday he was doing **drills** in the morning and taking **a military law class** in the afternoon.

(28) I didn't have any new **texts** from him when I got off the bus at **Pike Street**, so I figured we were still meeting at half-past four. I heard the music of **street buskers** a block away from the Market, and **on the sidewalks, baseball hats mixed with bright shirts, and hairy legs jutted out of jean shorts**. We wouldn't have normally gone near the Market and all its **trinket shops**, but on the lower level was a bookstore, which also **put out** a little magazine where I'd published an essay about our **stepbrother**, Chris. It was his birthday, and I was hoping the editor would give me a **copy**, for when Rob and I went to see him that night.

I hadn't met either of them in almost two years, and I wondered if Rob and I would resume the quarrelsome back and forth we'd kept up through high school, **if I'd** even recognize him. But then the **boiling** crowd parted, and, in front of the information booth, wearing **camo fatigues** and grinning into the sunlight, there he was.

(29) He took my hand, pulling me in, and clapped me on the back. "Hi, Danny. Hi, Danny-boy."

"**G.I. bro**." I stood back to **take in** his uniform. "It really is true."

It seemed like someone should be there to take a picture of us; it felt like the chapter where the characters come back together after so long, and the reader wonders how the years have changed things between them. But there was no reminiscing or exchange of

33 three hundred bucks:「300ドル」（buck はドルの通称）

34 cash:「（小切手を郵便局や銀行で）現金に換金する」

35 means:「収入、財産」

36 **Q. 3** これはどのようなことを言っているのでしょうか。discipline の意味を考えてみましょう。

37 Washington State: ワシントン州立大学の略称。ワシントン大学（州立）とは異なる。

38 grimy:「汚い」

off-campus:「大学キャンパスの外にある（主に学生向けの）」

bouncer:「用心棒（クラブやパブで迷惑客を追い払ったり、入り口で年齢確認をしたりする仕事）」

39 Reserves:「米軍の予備隊」

40 Basic Training: 米国陸軍の基礎訓練プログラム。

41 paralegal:「弁護士補助員（法律実務を行う資格はないが、一定の法律的仕事を行う訓練を受けている職）」

unit:「（予備隊の）部隊」

42 drills:「訓練」

43 a military law class:「軍法の授業」

44 texts:「テキストメッセージ、SMS」

45 Pike Street: シアトルの中心街の一つ。

46 street buskers:「ストリート・ミュージシャン」

46-48 on the sidewalks, baseball hats mixed with bright shirts, and hairy legs jutted out of jean shorts: 歩道を歩く人々の姿を描写している。

49 trinket shops:「みやげ物屋、小物屋」

50 put out:「出版する」

51 **Q. 4** stepbrother という言葉から何がわかりますか。

52 copy:「（雑誌、新聞、本の）1冊」

55 if I'd: [and wondered] if I would   boiling:「（群衆などが沸騰するように）激しく動く」

56-57 camo fatigues:「迷彩（カモフラージュ柄の）服」

60 G.I.:「軍人」   bro: brother の略   take in:「じっと見る」

61-62 **Q. 5** 「ぼく」はなぜこのように感じたのか考えてみましょう。

backstories, and instead, we plunged through the crowd and into the ₆₅ Market. We took the stairs down two floors, where the bookshop was wedged into a space next to a used record store. Inside, Rob read the titles of the volumes on the shelves, while I looked around the **frosted glass** partition, behind which a man was working on a computer. I was about to ask him where the magazine's editor was, but then the door ₇₀ opened and the woman who'd **commissioned** my essay walked in.

"Can I help you find something?" she said to Rob, who turned to face her.

(30) He stood straight and tall and had taken off his hat. "**No ma'am**."

"This is my brother," I said, and then I gave her my name. **The** ₇₅ **way she nodded**, I could tell she didn't understand who I was, though I'd sent an email saying I was coming. "I was wondering if there were **contributor** copies. Of the **latest issue**?"

"Right." She went into the back and came out with two magazines. "Sorry, I meant to reply to your message, but we've been buried with ₈₀ fall events, libraries, promotions. On and on. Would the two of you like a coffee? I was about to **step out**."

I stuffed the magazines into my backpack and said coffee sounded great. I didn't realize I'd been ignoring Rob until she held out her hand to him and said, "I'm Valerie, by the way." ₈₅

(31) Mom was right. My brother's time in the Army had left him thinner and there was **a fierce clarity** in his eyes as he looked at me from across the table. The coffee shop was next to the Market and the prices seemed to be a bad joke at first, but then the silent interior and serious, leather ₉₀ aprons of the staff turned the satire into tragedy. I hadn't eaten since breakfast, so I ordered a **fancy** turkey sandwich, hoping Valerie would pick up the check.

"You're in the Army?" she asked Rob.

"The Reserves," he said. "We had training today. I just haven't ₉₅ had a chance to **change**."

65 backstories:「裏話」

68-69 frosted glass:「曇りガラス」

71 commissioned:「依頼した」

74 ma'am: madam の省略形。

> **Q.6** この "No ma'am" という言い方に、ロブのどのような様子が見て取れるか考えてみましょう。

75-76 [From] the way she nodded:「彼女の頷いた様子から」

78 contributor:「寄稿者」

latest issue:「最新号」

82 step out:「(コーヒーを買いに)席を外す」

88 > **Q.7** a fierce clarityという言葉が兄のどのような様子を表しているか説明しましょう。

92 fancy:「高級な、高価な」

96 change:「着替える」

"You quit fishing?" Valerie asked as a barista brought over our coffees.

"No, you're thinking of my— of our stepbrother," I said. "His boat is up in **Ballard**." 100

"Oh, this is the magazine article you were talking about," Rob said to me. "Does Chris know you wrote about him?"

"I'm sure he remembers," I shrugged. After my parents' divorce, my mother had remarried to Chris' father, and Chris came to live on the farm and went to high school with Rob and me for two years 105 before **heading off to** mechanic's school. Then a year before, while I was **wasting away** at university, Valerie had visited my **creative writing class** and said she was putting together a special issue of her magazine called *Working Lives*. I'd interviewed Chris about being an engineer on a vessel that **fished the Bering Strait** and wrote it up for her. "I'm 110 taking him a copy. For his birthday."

100 Ballard: シアトル北西部のウォーターフロント地区。

106 heading off to:「～へ行く」

107 wasting away:「（時間などを）浪費する、無為に過ごす」

107-108 creative writing class:「（小説やエッセイなどの）創作の授業」

110 fished the Bering Strait:「ベーリング海峡で魚を捕った」この fish は他動詞で、「～で魚を捕る」の意。

🗨 **Expression**   本文を参考に次の表現を英語に直す時に空所に入る語を書きなさい。

1.   心配するな。

Don't (   ).

2.   君と私はお互いに助け合っていける。

You and I look (   ) each other.

3.   身の丈にあった生活をしなければいけない。

I have to live within my (   ).

4.   彼は教室を行ったり来たりした。

He went back and (   ) in the classroom.

5.   ちょうど私は彼に質問をしようとしていた。

I was (   ) to ask him.

💡 **Comprehension**   次の問いに答えなさい。

1.   My vision was charged with nervous energy (ℓ.3) とは、どのような様子をあらわしているでしょうか。

_____

2.   "You'll do fine. You and Rob look after each other." (ℓℓ.9-10) という父親のことばには、父親のどのような思いが込められていますか。

_____

3.   which underlined my own disquiet. (ℓℓ.11-12) とは、具体的に何によってどうなってしまったのですか。

_____

4.   I'd bombed my final exams, (ℓ.12) とは、どのようなことで、結果としてどうなりましたか。

_____

5.   I didn't have any new texts from him (ℓ.44) からどのようなことがわかったでしょうか。

_____

6. なぜいつもはマーケットやみやげ物屋に行かないのにふたりはその日は立ち寄ったのですか。

7. It seemed like someone should be there to take a picture of us. (ℓℓ.61-62) からどのような様子だったことがわかりますか。

8. On and on. (ℓ.81) からどのような様子がわかりますか。

9. I stuffed the magazines into my backpack and said coffee sounded great. (ℓℓ.83-84) の "coffee sounded great" とは、どのような意味でしょうか。

10. but then the silent interior and serious, leather aprons of the staff turned satire into tragedy. (ℓℓ.90-91) のように風刺劇が悲劇になったのはなぜですか。

⇄ Discussion

1. ロブのその後の生活がどのようなものであったか、話し合ってみましょう。

2. 義兄弟のクリスはロブやダンとどういう関係にあるのか、話し合ってみましょう。

✏️ Writing

Would you like to write an essay about someone you know? Why or why not?

Grammar Guide —— 名詞節を導く接続詞の if

[I] didn't know if I could stay focused or keep my grades up.（ℓℓ.16-17）では if 以下
の節は know の目的語となっています。 この場合の if は「かどうか」で、whether とほぼ同義
です。「私が集中力を保って、成績を維持できるかどうか、わからなかった。」の意味になります。
I wondered if Rob and I would resume the quarrelsome...（ℓℓ.53-54）も同様の if です。
if は「もし」だけではないので注意が必要です。

Unit: 11

アメリカを中心とする有志連合がイラク戦争に突入するのが2003年で、戦争の終結は2003年5月に宣言されていますので、56-58行目の記述から、物語のこの部分はイラク戦争から2年後の2005年であることが分かります。

📖 Pre-reading

1. イチローとシアトル・マリナーズを調べてみましょう。

2. Taliban, Bush, Iraqからどのような戦争の話なのか、調べてみましょう。

🎙 Vocabulary

次の語の定義を下記のaからjの中から選びなさい。

1. salute	**2.** wipe	**3.** aptitude	**4.** insurgency	**5.** inferno
6. freak	**7.** uncanny	**8.** threat	**9.** stumble	**10.** descend

a. to rub a surface with something in order to remove dirt, liquid etc.

b. to become suddenly angry or afraid, especially so that you cannot control your behavior

c. an attempt by a group of people to take control of their government using force and violence

d. an extremely large and dangerous fire – used especially in news reports

e. very strange and difficult to explain

f. to move your right hand to your head, especially in order to show respect to an officer in the army, navy etc.

g. to move from a higher level to a lower one

h. to hit your foot against something or put your foot down awkwardly while you are walking or running, so that you almost fall

i. natural ability or skill, especially in learning

j. a statement in which you tell someone that you will cause them harm or trouble if they do not do what you want

(32) "**I**t was an interesting piece," Valerie said.

Rob said, "Well, I hope he likes it."

"Why wouldn't he like it?"

"People see themselves their own way," he said. "But then someone—you come and tell them something different. They might ⁵ not like the way you see it."

Valerie shook her head. "But on the other hand, you **canonize** them forever in your writing."

Like her, **there were few things I could imagine more exciting than** seeing my name on a book or reading about myself in its pages. ¹⁰ To be even a minor character in a **Denis Johnson** story or mentioned in the **acknowledgments** of a **Zadie Smith** novel would have been **worth the price of a major organ**, though I could tell by Rob's expression this **accounting** didn't **add up** to him.

"Canonize them?" He laughed and looked from Valerie to me. ¹⁵ "You book people are so weird."

A silence fell over us, and after a minute, Valerie polished off her coffee, saying, "I've got to get back. Book people stuff. This should cover me."

(33) She put a ten-dollar bill on the table and disappeared out the ²⁰ door. I **shot** Rob **a look**, but he just said, "What?" After I paid the remainder of the check and tipped, I only had eight bucks. We left the café, **heading for** the bus stop. The setting sun had turned **Elliot Bay** into a pool of **molten** silver, and Rob was texting Chris, looking at his phone as we crossed the street. I heard someone shout, "Hey **private**. ²⁵ Hey there."

I figured it was some tourist, but when I turned a black man was coming toward us in a blue polo shirt, and Rob **knocked his heels together as he saluted**. "Yes, **Major**."

(34) The man told Rob to be at ease, and I introduced myself as his ³⁰ brother. He said, "I was just walking down to the stadium, trying to get a ticket for the game. See Ichiro play."

7 canonize:「聖者のように人々の記憶に残る人物として描く」 元々は、キリスト教の文脈で、死者を聖者の列に加えることを意味するが、文学用語としては、ある作家や作品を正典に含める、つまり文学史上の重要作家や作品として位置づけることを、しばしば意味する。日常ではあまり使われないjargon（専門用語）なので、文学に興味の無いロブには理解できていない。

9-10 **Q. 1** ここではfewとmore〜thanという比較級が一文の中で使われていますが、この箇所を文法的に正確に日本語に訳すとどのようになるか考えてみましょう。

11 Denis Johnson: デニス・ジョンソン（1949-2017） アメリカの作家。*Jesus' Son*などの作品で知られる。

12 acknowledgments:「謝辞」

Zadie Smith: ゼイディー・スミス（1975-） イギリスの作家。*White Teeth*などの作品で知られる。

12-13 worth the price of:「〜の価値がある」

13 a major organ:「身体の主要な臓器」

14 accounting:「計算」

add up:「（主に否定文で）計算が合う」

17-19 **Q. 2** 直前のロブの発言とそれに対するヴァレリーの反応を考え、この場の雰囲気について考えてみましょう。

17 polish off:「食べ物などをさっと片付ける、食べてしまう」の意。

19 cover:「（金額が）まかなう、足りる」

21 shot ... a look:「（人に）視線を投げつけた、睨みつけた」

23 heading for: heading [for, to〜]で、「〜へ向かう」の意味。ing形で使われることが多い。

Elliot Bay:「エリオット湾」ピュージェット湾の一部で、シアトルに臨む。

24 molten:「溶けた」

25 private:「二等兵（陸軍で一番下の階級の兵士の呼称）」

28-29 **Q. 3** ロブの体の動きを具体的に想像してみましょう。

29 Major:「少佐（陸軍で上位の階級）」

To me, Rob said, "Major Peers is in **JAG Corps**. He taught the law seminar today."

"You live in the city?" I asked. ₃₅

"No, they put me up in a hotel." Pinheads of sweat stood out on his brow, and he wiped them with a handkerchief. "This place is too expensive. A taxi here costs as much as buying a car should. I'm from Milwaukee, but I got a place on **Ft. Lewis** now."

"Are the Reserve units on base preparing to **deploy**?" Rob asked. ₄₀

"Some are." Major Peers glanced at me. "And what about you? The private tells me both your parents were in the service. **We going** to **talk you into joining up**?"

"Not me," I said. "Don't think I have the right, well, the right **aptitude**." ₄₅

He laughed. "**Nothing a good** drill **sergeant** couldn't **straighten out**."

"Major, have you heard of any **activated** units with spots for—"

"Ah, not my **jurisdiction**," he said, turning from us. "I'll let you boys be on your way." ₅₀

⁽₃₅⁾ We watched the Major walk away, and as I followed Rob to the bus stop, I asked him what he'd wanted to know about deploying, but he didn't answer. We reached the avenue, and when the **Fremont-bound** bus **pulled up**, we got on and sat in the back.

When I'd heard Rob was joining the Reserves, I wasn't worried. ₅₅ **The Taliban** had been defeated and it was two years since **Bush** had landed on an **aircraft carrier** and declared Iraq to be "Mission Accomplished." Troops were coming home, and no reserve units would be **called up**. But **since then, the insurgency had turned Iraq into an inferno**, and the generals **were convinced** the solution was to throw as ₆₀ many young people onto the **pyre** as possible.

"Mom and Dad are **freaked out** you know. They're worried you'll be sent."

"I know," he said. "They changed our unit's status from inactive

33 JAG Corps[=Judge Advocate General's]: 陸軍の法務部門。

39 Ft. Lewis: ワシントン州タコマ市にあった陸軍の駐屯地。Ft. は Fort（砦）の略。

40 deploy:「配置につく」

42 We going: be 動詞が省略されていて、[Are] we going の意。

43 talk you into:「（人を）説得して～させる」

joining up:「（軍に）入隊する」

45 aptitude:「適性」

46 Nothing a good ... : = [There is] nothing a good ...

sergeant:「軍曹」

46-47 straighten out:「真っ直ぐにする、鍛える」

48 activated:「実戦に関わる軍務につくよう命令を受けた」

49 jurisdiction:「管轄」

53 Fremont:「フレモント」（シアトル市内の街区の地名）

-bound:「～行きの」

54 pulled up:「停まった」

56 The Taliban: 主にアフガニスタンを拠点とするイスラム教スンニ派の過激派組織。
Bush: 第43代合衆国大統領 ジョージ・W・ブッシュ (George W. Bush, 1946-) 2001年
9月11日の同時多発テロと、合衆国のイラク侵攻が行われた時の大統領。

57 aircraft carrier:「航空母艦」

59 called up:「招集された」

59-60 since then, the insurgency had turned Iraq into an inferno: 米軍の撤退によって、
反乱が勃発し、イラク国内の政情が劇的に悪化したことを inferno と表現している。

60 were convinced:「～と確信していた」that をこのあとに補って考える。

61 pyre:「（特に火葬用の）薪の山」

62 freaked out:「気も狂わんばかりだ」

Unit: 11

to **on-alert**, but don't tell them. I still don't think we'll go." 65

"Good." The **one uncanny bit of luck** in all this was that Rob had been assigned to a **chemical weapons disposal unit**, and while the administration and its media allies had been **bludgeoning** their opponents with the threat of **WMDs** for years, there was, in fact, nothing for them to do over there. 70

"I **volunteered for activation**," he said. "If there's a space with another unit, I'll deploy."

"What?" The other bus passengers looked at me, and I realized I'd almost shouted. "Why would you do something like that?"

"Our country's at war. Someone has to fight it." 75

(36) A boy I'd been friends with in high school had been deployed a year before. He'd been in south **Baghdad**, following a copper **trip wire** that **his platoon thought** had triggered a bomb, when a second **IED** blew him into the air. They said the facial wounds made his body unrecognizable. 80

"You heard about Justin?" I said, and Rob nodded. "And what was the point?"

"I don't know," he said. "But this is what I'm doing."

(37) We got off the bus and walked over the **Ballard Bridge** toward **Fishermen's** 85 **Terminal**. The light was almost gone, but I took out a copy of the magazine and **flipped** to the article. I started reading aloud my description of what Chris had said about snow falling on **the Arctic Ocean**, which I'd only slightly **fictionalized** by **making it at night** and having a pale seabird cross the sky. 90

To Rob's back, I said, "You think he wouldn't like this?"

"**Would** a bird fly in a snowstorm?"

"It's just a detail," I said. "Where are we going?"

"They're at this place up ahead, but they're heading back to the boat." 95

When I looked up, we were nearing a sign in the shape of a

65 on-alert:「派兵待機」

66 one uncanny bit of luck: イラクが所有するはずの化学兵器などを含む大量破壊兵器の脅威を取り除くことがイラク派兵の名目だったが、実際には大量破壊兵器が見つからなかったため、ロブが所属する化学兵器処理部隊が現場で任務につく可能性は低いことを、「不可解な幸運」と呼んでいる。

67 chemical weapons disposal unit:「化学兵器処理部隊」

68 bludgeoning:「棍棒で叩く、激しく非難する」

69 WMDs: weapons of mass destruction（大量破壊兵器）の略。核兵器のほか、生物兵器、化学兵器などのことを指す。

71 volunteered for activation:「実戦に関わる軍務に志願した」

77 Baghdad:「バグダッド」イラクの首都。

77-78 trip wire:「（地雷などを起動させる）仕掛け線」

78 his platoon thought:「彼の小隊が考えるところによれば（一種の挿入句）」

79 IED: improvised explosive device（即席爆発装置）の略。

85 Ballard Bridge: シアトルにある跳ね橋。

85-86 Fishermen's Terminal: シアトルの主に漁船向けの港。

87 flipped:「ページをめくった」

88 The Arctic Ocean:「北極海」

89 fictionalized:「フィクションにした、創作を加えた」

> **Q. 4** making it at nightのitは何を指しているでしょうか？

92 **Q. 5** なぜwouldが使われているのか、文法的に意味を説明してみましょう。

cowboy boot, glowing with neon letters that read *The Kickin' Cowboy Restaurant & **Saloon***. Chris didn't answer when Rob called from the parking lot, but the door opened and a man walked out singing in a foreign language to the tune of happy birthday. Chris came out high 100 stepping like a **drum major** in a marching band. When he saw Rob and me standing in the dark he came over and wrapped us in big **bear hugs** one after another.

"**Doughboy** Rob. Dan the man," he said, then gestured behind him. "This is my captain, Pehr. Come with us to the dock." 105

Rob walked in front, talking to Chris about when he'd be shipping out next. We crossed the road and came to the docks, where hundreds of boats bobbed in the water, their masts swaying like **denuded** trees. As he stumbled along, I asked the captain where he was from.

"Small city, near the Russian border. Two **tours** Finland Navy 110 and now how many decades fishing Alaska? Salmon, crab, everything I catch. Shark, giant squid, sea monster, all of it I catch." He grinned madly and raised a fist in the air as we descended a metal **gangplank** onto a wide concrete dock. On either side of us, enormous vessels rocked in the night, giants shifting in their sleep. He walked on ahead 115 of me, passing by where Rob and Chris had come to a stop beside one of the towering hulls, and skipped up a set of portable stairs, like the kind you **wheel** up to an airplane, climbing on to the deck of the ship. "But tonight my tour is ended. **Öitä!**"

98   *Saloon*:「酒場、バー」

101   drum major:「楽隊長」

102   bear hug:「強い抱擁」

104   Doughboy:（第一次世界大戦時の）米軍歩兵の通称、広く兵士一般を指す呼称としても使われる。

108   denuded:「丸裸の」

110   tours:「軍隊の勤務期間」

113   gangplank:「（船の）タラップ」

118   wheel:「（下に車輪が付いているものを）押して動かす」

119   Öitä: フィンランド語で夜（あるいは、おやすみ）の意。

💬 **Expression**　　本文を参考に次の表現を英語に直す時に空所に入る語を書きなさい。

1.　友だちといるとすっかりくつろげる。

　　I can feel (　　　　　　　) ease with friends.

2.　彼らが入隊するように説得するだろう。

　　They are going to talk you (　　　　　　　) joining up.

3.　そろそろ行くよ。

　　I'll be (　　　　　　　) my way.

4.　バスがデパートの横に停まった。

　　The bus pulled (　　　　　　　) at the department store.

5.　私はコンピュータ部門に配属された。

　　I was assigned (　　　　　　　) the computer section.

💡 **Comprehension**　　次の問いに答えなさい。

1.　"Why wouldn't he like it?" (ℓ.3) のこのダンの発言とそれに対するロブの答えから、ダンとロブの考え方の違いを説明してみましょう。

2.　"you canonize them forever in your writing." (ℓℓ.7-8) の文の意味をわかりやすく説明してください。

3.　This should cover me. (ℓℓ.18-19) の This を明らかにして意味を説明してください。

4.　ロブの言った "What?" (ℓ.21) と I only had eight bucks. (ℓ.22) には、どのような関連がありますか。

5. The setting sun had turned Elliot Bay into a pool of molten silver, (ℓℓ.23-24) とは、どのような情景ですか。

6. 少佐の言った "Nothing a good drill sergeant couldn't straighten out." (ℓℓ.46-47) はどのようなことを意味していますか。

7. and the generals were convinced the solution was to throw as many young people onto the pyre as possible. (ℓℓ.60-61) とは、具体的にどのようなことを指していますか。

8. "Why would you do something like that?" (ℓ.74) に込められた気持ちを説明しなさい。

9. 戦死したジャスティンのことを聞いたロブの態度はどのようなものでしたか。

10. "Would a bird fly in a snowstorm?" (ℓ.92) では、どのようなことを言いたかったのですか。

⇄ Discussion

1. ダンとロブの再会の様子がどのように変わってきたかを話し合ってみましょう。

2. クリスとの再会の様子を話し合ってみましょう。

✎ Writing

Write a letter of appointment to go and see your friend, your family, etc.

_____

_____

_____

_____

_____

_____

_____

_____

_____

_____

_____

_____

_____

Grammar Guide —— 直接法の if 　未来に起こりうることを表します。

"If there's a space with another unit, I'll deploy." (ℓℓ.71-72) 将来的にありえることを述べる場合は仮定法ではなく、直接法を用いて表現します。「もし、他の部隊に空きがあれば、私が配置につきます」では、ifで始まる副詞節では未来のことを指していますが未来形を使わずに現在形で代用し、主節は未来形で表現されます。

Unit : 12

いよいよ兄と弟の物語も最後の場面を迎えます。義兄弟に会ったあとで、バスに乗り遅れたふたりがどうしたかをお互いの感情を考えながら追ってみましょう。

Pre-reading

1. frosted cookieはどのようなお菓子でしょうか、調べてみましょう。

2. ベーリング海峡とそこでの漁業についてどのようなものか、調べてみましょう。

Vocabulary

次の語の定義を下記のaからjの中から選びなさい。

1. state-of-the-art	**2.** miraculous	**3.** tear	**4.** stuff	**5.** frown
6. trudge	**7.** dissolve	**8.** brace	**9.** plunge	**10.** soak

a. used when you are talking about things such as substances, materials, or groups of objects when you do not know what they are called, or it is not important to say exactly what they are

b. to mix with a liquid and become part of it

c. using the most modern and recently developed methods, materials, or knowledge

d. to mentally or physically prepare yourself or someone else for something unpleasant that is going to happen

e. to move, fall, or be thrown suddenly forwards or downwards

f. to make a hole in something by force

g. to keep it covered with a liquid for a period of time, especially in order to make it softer or easier to clean

h. to walk with slow heavy steps, especially because you are tired or it is difficult to walk

i. very good, completely unexpected, and often very lucky

j. to make an angry, unhappy, or confused expression, moving your eyebrows together

⟨39⟩ From two stories above us, **he** waved and then disappeared behind the **gunwale**. Chris was leaning against what I now recognized as his truck.

"He said goodnight in Finnish."

"This is your boat?" Rob asked. 5

"The Northern **Jaeger**. Three-hundred feet of **state-of-the-art** fish processing."

"What's a jaeger?"

"**Means** hunter in German." I shrugged when Rob looked at me. "I looked it up for the article." I took a copy of the magazine out 10 of my backpack and handed it to Chris, telling him happy birthday. "Remember, it's just my interpretation."

"Wait, wait. I got something, too," Rob said, digging in the **cargo pocket** of his camo pants. He came out with an oversized **frosted** cookie, which was miraculously in one piece. "See, **I got them to write** 15 **your name**. I didn't have any candles, so…"

⟨40⟩ He pulled out a box of matches. It wouldn't stay lit long, so we didn't sing, and Chris held the cookie in his hand, while Rob struck the match and pressed it down into the frosting. Chris blew it out, laughing to himself, but he **wouldn't** tell us what he'd wished for. He put down 20 the **tailgate** of his truck and we sat on it as he tore the cookie into three pieces and handed them around.

Rob asked, "You like working on the boat?"

"I'm not sure I like it, but it suits me." He looked at the ship's bridge, **towering above**. "It's like the Army. Everyone has a rank, you 25 wake up at a certain time, you have your job, take care of your stuff, and if you do a good job you **move up**."

Rob said. "I enjoy a routine. In Basic Training, my eyes opened five minutes before they called out the wake-up. **You got so you could move without thinking**. It was in your blood." 30

I said, "I like to work. **Don't** mind staying up all night even. But mornings are my weakness."

1　he: Unit 11の最後に登場した船長を指す。

2　gunwale:「船べり」

6　Jaeger:「トウゾクカモメ」(ここではThe Northern Jaegerは船の名前。「北のかもめ号」といったところ。)

　　state-of-the-art:「最先端の」

9　Means: [It] means

13-14　cargo pocket:「カーゴパンツのポケット」

14　frosted:「砂糖をまぶした」

15-16　**Q.1**　このthemは誰のことを指していますか？

20　wouldn't:「どうしても～しようとしなかった」

21　tailgate: トラックの荷台の後部開閉板。

25　towering above:「高くそびえ立って」

27　move up:「昇進する」

29-30　You got so you could move without thinking:「考えずに動くことができるようになった」の意。主語 ＋ get so ＋ 主語 ＋ can ＋ 動詞で、「～できるようになる」の意。しばしば過去形で用いられる。

31　Don't: = [I] don'tの意。口語の会話では主語が省略されることはしばしばある。

Chris said, "Different kinds of work though. **Working** with your hands, you can't be doing it late, when you're tired. You lose a finger like that. It's best when you wake up. You're alert. Ready." 35

"That's what I miss about the Army. Working, moving, and you meet people from all over."

"Did you tell him you volunteered for deployment?" Chris asked, and I **shook my head with unhappiness**. "I never understood how you two **wound up** being nothing alike." 40

(41) It turned out Rob and I had to leave to **make** the last bus before they switched to the night schedule, so we said goodbye to Chris, who would sleep on the ship. We hadn't gone far when Rob looked over his shoulder, said hurry up, and then started jogging. By the time we 45 reached the street where the **stop** was, we were sprinting; we got there just in time to see the bus **pull away**.

"We **should've** left earlier," I said.

"You couldn't run any faster?"

"**Whatever**." The streets around there were deserted. "When's the 50 next one?"

Rob tapped at his phone and frowned. "More than an hour. I don't have enough for a cab. If you pay, I'll give you cash tomorrow."

I told him I was **tapped out**. "I guess we're walking. **Nice plan**."

His map said it was an hour and a half walk to his apartment in 55 **Belltown**. We **trudged** along without talking until a light rain started. Rob said, "Let's cut through the park up here."

(42) Trees hung over a **chain-link** fence that ran along the trail, and they gave us some **respite**, but then the rain thickened. We stopped beneath the **fronds** of a **cedar**, which **dribbled** the occasional stream of 60 cold water onto my neck but otherwise provided cover.

"How much did you say you had?" Rob yelled over the storm.

"Eight bucks and a check from Mom."

"A check? Let me see. Maybe we can cash it."

33　Working: 分詞構文で、[When you are] workingの意。

39　**Q.2**　どのような意味合いでダンは首を振っているのでしょうか？

40　wound up: wind up ~ingで、結局~することになる。

42　make:「間に合う」

46　stop:「バス停」

47　pull away:「出発する」

48　should've: should haveの省略形。

50　Whatever:「なんでも良いけどさ」といった意味の間投詞。

54　tapped out:「すっからかんで、一文無しで」

　　Nice plan: これは皮肉で言っている。

56　Belltown: シアトルの街の地名。

　　trudged:「トボトボ歩いた」

58　chain-link:「網の目状の」

59　respite:「休息」ここでは「雨がかからないこと（雨宿り）」を意味している。

60　fronds:「（シダなどの）葉」

　　cedar:「ヒマラヤ杉」

　　dribbled:「滴らせた」

"I don't want to get it wet," I shouted back. 65

"Give it to me **already**."

I took out my wallet, handing over the check, and he examined it with the light of his phone. Transparent circles formed on the paper as raindrops landed on it. It was all I had until I found a job.

"Here, give it back," I reached for the check, but when he let it go, 70 the wind blew it into the darkness beyond the fence.

(43) I pressed my face into the chain links. The soaked paper was caught in a branch, and I shoved my sneakers into the gaps of the fence and jumped over. As my eyes adjusted, I realized the ground **fell away** after only a few feet; the trees grew **at an angle** from the hill. I **braced** 75 **myself against** the cedar's trunk and stretched out my arm, but the check was beyond my fingertips. **Why did he still, after all these years, not listen?** But I could almost touch it. I heard Rob's boots land on the other side of the fence behind me. I reached out again, further, and the check folded into my grasp. 80

"Wait," Rob said too late, and I plunged face-first down the hill, like I was spinning in a washing machine—three, four—I lost count. A **fern broke my fall**, but in the next instant, Rob crashed into me from behind.

(44) For a while, we sat there at the bottom of the slope. The check 85 wasn't in my hand anymore. Slowly my vision dissolved the darkness, and I realized a man was watching us. He stood outside a **tattered** tent, and the hood of his jacket dripped as he smoked a cigarette in the rain.

"I twisted my ankle," Rob said.

My teeth were **gritty**, and I spat. I looked into the **pitch-black** 90 behind us and felt the massive **presence** of the slope. Already my money was gone, vanished, and **under my breath, I cursed this city, which had defeated me once before, where my luck always ran out**.

"What?" Rob said. I looked at his serious, dark features **streaked** with dirt, his lip swelling up like an injured cartoon character. I **giggled** 95 and covered my mouth, but I couldn't help it. Again, he asked, "What?"

66　already:「早く、すぐに」

74　fell away:「（土地が急傾斜で）下がっている」

75　at an angle:「斜めに」

75-76　braced myself against:「体をもたせかける」

77-78　**Q. 3**　ここから語り手の兄に対するどのような感情を読み取ることができるでしょうか。

83　fern broke my fall:「シダが落下の衝撃を和らげてくれた」（break one's fallで、～を落下から助けるの意。ここでは文字通りの意味だが、比喩的に～を救う、の意味でもよく使われる。）

87　tattered:「ぼろぼろの」

90　gritty:「砂利っぽい、砂利で口の中がジャリジャリする」

　　pitch-black:「真っ暗闇」

91　presence:「存在感」

92　under my breath:「聞こえないぐらいの小さな声で」

92-93　**Q. 4**　ここで"had defeated me once"というのは、具体的にどのようなことを意味しているでしょうか？

94　streaked:「縞模様のついた」

95　giggled:「クスクスと笑った」

I caught my breath. "We fall halfway to hell, and you want to know 'what'? God, you're **thick**."

"At least I'm not some dumb **klutz**."

I **lost it** again, but then I felt the homeless man giving us the eye. 100 Rob struggled to his feet.

(45) We were an hour from his apartment, the rain hadn't **let up**, and I didn't even know if he could walk. We were soaked, covered in mud, far from home; we were poor, failed creatures, like so many in that miserable night. But I put an arm around him until he was steady, and 105 we faced the dark hill together, as brothers.

98 thick:「頭がぼうっとした、鈍い」

99 klutz:「のろま、大ばか」

100 lost it:「自制心を失った、カッとなった」

102 let up:「（雨などが）止んだ」

Expression　本文を参考に次の表現を英語に直す時に空所に入る語を書きなさい。

1. それで問題ありません。

   That would (　　　　　　) me fine.

2. お気をつけて。

   Take (　　　　　　) of yourself.

3. アイツのことは気にするな。

   Don't (　　　　　　) him.

4. もっと早く起きるべきだった。

   I should (　　　　　　) gotten up earlier.

5. 雨が小降りになった。

   The rain (　　　　　　) up.

Comprehension　次の問いに答えなさい。

1. "Remember, it's just my interpretation." (ℓ.12) とあらかじめことわりを入れたのはなぜですか。

2. ロブは軍隊での生活にどんな価値を見出していましたか。それがわかる箇所を抜き出し、説明しなさい。

3. クリスは手を使う仕事はどうしたら良いと言っていますか。

4. I told him I was tapped out. (ℓ.54) とは、どのような経過でこのようになったのでしょうか。

5. ..., but otherwise provided cover. (ℓ.61) の otherwise の内容を明らかにして意味を説明しなさい。

6. It was all I had until I found a job. (ℓ.69) のItの内容を明らかにして意味を説明しなさい。

7. Why did he still, after all these years, not listen? (ℓℓ.77-78) の指す内容は何ですか。

8. I cursed this city, (ℓ.92) とありますがどうしてなのですか。

9. "We fall halfway to hell, and you want to know 'what'? God, you're thick." (ℓℓ.97-98) と言った「ぼく」の気持ちを説明しなさい。

10. we were poor, failed creatures, like so many in that miserable night. (ℓℓ.104-105) とは、どのようなことを指しているでしょうか。

⇄ Discussion

1. クリスの言った "I never understood how you two wound up being nothing alike." (ℓℓ.39-40) の理由を話し合ってみましょう。

2. we faced the dark hill together, as brothers. (ℓ.106) について、このときの語り手の心情を話し合ってみましょう。

✎ Writing

Describe the most impressive part in the whole story and explain why you chose it.

_____

_____

_____

_____

_____

_____

_____

_____

_____

_____

_____

Grammar Guide — 接続詞 but

　物語の後半になって、I lost it again, but then I felt the homeless man giving us the eye.（ℓ.100）But I put an arm around him until he was steady,（ℓ.105）のように接続詞のbutが用いられています。butは通常は逆接の意味が多いのですが、ここでは前の表現から期待される当然の成り行きではなく、個人的な見解や心で思ったこと、視点が変わっていることの指標として用いられています。前段を受けた、「しかし」ではなく「でも、さて」という意味として捉えると良いでしょう。

著者略歴

Michael Larson

Michael Larson lives in Tokyo and teaches English and American literature at Keio University. After graduating from Dartmouth College, he completed his PhD at the University of Wisconsin-Milwaukee and received a Fulbright Grant to research the 2011 Tohoku Earthquake and Tsunami in Japan, later writing a nonfiction account of the disaster *When the Waves Came: Loss, Recovery, and the Great Tohoku Earthquake and Tsunami* (Chin Music Press 2020).

編著者

日本英文学会関東支部

奥聡一郎（関東学院大学）

久世恭子（東洋大学）

笹川　渉（青山学院大学）

佐藤和哉（日本女子大学）

古屋耕平（青山学院大学）

教室の英文学シリーズ Vol. 1「兄と弟の記録」

2023年1月31日　初版第1刷発行

著　者	Michael Larson
編　者	日本英文学会（関東支部）
発行者	小川　洋一郎
発行所	株式会社　朝日出版社
	〒101-0065 東京都千代田区西神田3-3-5
	TEL：03-3239-0271　FAX：03-3239-0479
	E-MAIL：text-e@asahipress.com
	https://www.asahipress.com/
印　刷	錦明印刷株式会社
DTP	イーズ

ISBN978-4-255-15703-0